SAGAR SAGA

To:
My wife Carole
who pushed me to finish this second volume
despite other priorities


and to:
the late Dora Scarlett (1905 – 2001)
who inspired me at
Seva Nilayam

All royalties from this volume will be donated to
Village Service Trust
which still supports her work.

# Sagar Saga 2

A young volunteer's discovery of
Post-colonial India

A trilogy:

Volume 2: summer 1968
The big trip South

ISBN 979-10-96332-03-8

# Map of India showing outline route

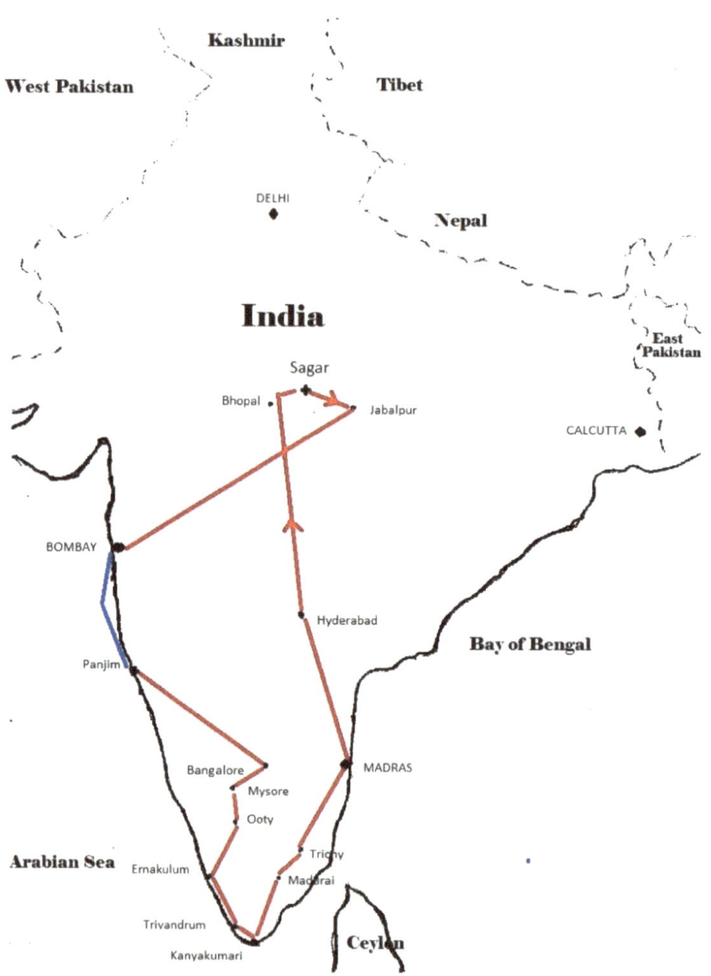

# CONTENTS


## Sagar – the context

1. And off I went to the bus-stand in a tonga… 1

## Heading South – Middle class India

2. Return to Bombay 5
3. From Bombay to Goa 15
4. On to Bangalore 28
5. Arrival in Kerala 35
6. Elephant hunt 42
7 Shibili and co 49
8. Trivandrum 55
9. Land's End -Kanyakumari 59

## Heading North - Volunteer India

10. Boys' Town and well-boring 67
11. Seva Nilayam 83
12. Madurai 92
13. Kodaikanal 96
14. Trichy 100
15. Madras High Life 103
16. Hyderabad Public School 111
17. Home again, home again, jiggety-jig! 118
    A note on illustrations 120

# Sagar – the context

## 1 And off I went to the bus-stand in a tonga...

...thus ends the first volume of *Sagar Saga.*

It was the 2nd May 1968, the afternoon was hot and I was 22 years old.  I clambered up into the two-wheeled horse-drawn vehicle which still served as taxi in this part of India.  My old cook and manservant Lalgi handed me the small padlocked metal suitcase and canvas haversack which friends had lent me.  These contained all I thought I needed for the next 10 weeks.  Strapped to the case was the yellow check cotton bedspread – borrowed from my University rooms - which would serve me as bedding and sometimes as bed.

"Ram Ram, sahib," he said, folding his hands together and bowing.  "Be careful now, gentleman!  I look after quarters, gentleman."

Bending out from my rear-facing seat in the tonga, I returned his farewell, adding, "See you in July, Lalgi!"

The tonga-wallah turned round.

"Tik hé, sahib?  Bus-stand jayengé?"

"Han, bus-stand chelengé!"

He gave his undernourished horse a flick of the whip, we both settled as far back under the canvas awning as we could, and off we trotted from the small apartment in the University Guest House where I had lived for the last few months.


Since August, I had been working at the University of Sagar in Madhya Pradesh (Hindi for "Middle State" – approximately the old Central Provinces of the British Raj).

Depending on one's point of view, I was a young British volunteer trying to make himself useful in India, an unwitting foot-soldier of European neo-colonialism, a white sahib deserving exaggerated respect and systematic over-charging or a fully-fledged Assistant Professor of English with prestigious European qualifications.

Midway between the major cities of Bhopal and Jabalpur, Sagar, just north of the Tropic of Cancer at 23° 50' N, 78° 44' E, had been the geographic centre of "British" India – a remote district headquarters with a large military encampment, surrounded by Kipling's jungle and a sprinkling of small former princely states. The old town was medieval and its fort had in the early 19th century been a centre for the suppression of the Thugs – those murderous sects of ritual highway robbers – some of whom, I was told, had been crucified at the entrances to the town. Dacoits or bandits still roamed the countryside around, occasionally kidnapping for ransom or killing the odd policeman. The only industry was the production of *bidis* – that strong and popular cross between a small cigarette and a smaller cigar, sold in its distinctive cone-shaped paper packet.

The population - about 100,000 at the time, much more now - was predominantly Hindu, with a large Muslim minority and a tiny Christian one. As for Europeans, there was a convent school run by German nuns, a church run by a couple of Swedish missionaries, the 65-year-old Professor of Geology at the University – and me.

The University had been founded in 1946, one year before Independence by Sir Hari Singh Gour, a local son who had made good and donated his family wealth to provide education for the people of this under-developed region. It was still very new in 1967 and in a rapid phase of expansion which made its hilltop campus overlooking the town resemble a sprawling building site. Some of the departments had a national reputation and were involved in important original research – the Pharmacy and Geology Departments immediately come to mind. The main work of the English Department, however, was to teach English Literature and Criticism to graduate students, very few of whom had any interest in the subject. The vast majority were

South Indians from Kerala – several days away by train - who had first degrees in Science, but had failed to get into graduate programmes in their own subjects or nearer home.

My work was uninspiring. I had never wanted to be an academic and didn't really see how the teaching of Keats' Odes contributed to the post-colonial development of a newly independent country. I – and VSO who sent me – believed that I would be teaching English as a Second Language and I had received some practical training in this. But my head of department, Professor Mohan Lal thought I was much too valuable to be wasted on teaching people to communicate in the international language. Instead, I gave desultory lectures on Eng. Lit. for a few hours a week, often keeping just a few pages ahead of the students. Oh yes, and my A-level French allowed Mohan Lal to justify the "and Modern European Languages" in his department's title by setting up a Beginner's Diploma course in that language.

My timetable was light and was made even lighter by the many holidays – both scheduled and unscheduled – and by frequent student strikes. In short, I was not professionally fulfilled.

On the other hand, my social life was enjoyable. I quickly made many friends amongst both staff and students. As there was no expatriate community to be drawn into, I went through a process of what my Indian friends referred to as "Indianization" or what most expats would have called "going native". I took advantage of the many breaks to travel, and was invited to the homes of friends in what they called the "real India" of small towns and remote villages. I also directed an unforgettable production of *Macbeth* – interpret that as you will and go buy a copy of Volume One!

Now the hot weather had really set in, exams were over, the students had dispersed to their homes – mainly in South India – and the university was closing down until mid-July.

My southern students had insisted for months that I should visit them in Kerala (their "real India", which they assured me was a cleaner, greener and better organized land than the former Central Provinces) and I had accepted their invitation, ignoring the warnings from some northern colleagues that I was asking for trouble as southerners were utterly unreliable...  It was arranged that my student Mathew John (an evangelical Christian – hence the un-Indian name) would meet me off the train at Ernakulum on or around the 15th, final details to be fixed by telegram.  He would liaise with other students to arrange my onward tour.

Kerala was to be the only part of the voyage which was planned in advance. For the rest, I would improvise.  I was armed with a few letters of introduction friends had given me to relatives and friends in the southern states and with a list of addresses of VSO volunteers in South India and Ceylon furnished by the British Council in Bombay.  I forgot that Ceylon was a separate country and inadvertently torpedoed my chance of going there by leaving my passport behind for safe keeping.  So I set out with no official ID, no credit cards, oh and if you can imagine this, no mobile phone!

What I did have was my red *Ganga Diary,* which I wrote up almost every day.  That and letters home are the bases of the following pages.

# Heading South – Middle class India

## 2. Return to Bombay

So there I was in the tonga thinking of the year that had passed and looking forward with a mixture of excitement and unease to the weeks ahead.

We rattled through the heat of the deserted campus, our wooden wheels clattering on the uneven tarmac.  We drove past the monumental Library in whose conference hall we had produced *Macbeth* and I had rolled helplessly round the stage in my caldron, clutching my apparitions; past the coffee shop where I had hidden in a back room while my mentor, Vijay Chauhan got rid of an importunate student who was harassing me to be "understanding" and remark his appalling French exam paper; past the pumping station which supplied the University with water for two hours every morning and two hours every evening.

We trundled out through the University Gateway onto the winding road which snakes its way down the hill to the city. Here the horse became recalcitrant, deciding it was going to walk on the softer verge beside the road – more comfortable for its hooves, but not for the tonga's narrow wheels.  A battle of wills ensued between horse and driver and we swerved on and off the road for the next few minutes.

At the bottom of the hill we drove between the old colonial bungalows of Civil Lines, with their thick walls, surrounding verandas and thatched roofs, past n° 8, where my friend and young colleague Saeed Ali lived with his widowed mother,  an excellent cook,  past n° 10, home of Munna Chauhan's in-laws and their student lodger, my friend Shukla aka Macbeth.  And on through the outskirts of town, down to the huge lake which gave Sagar its name.

Here we turned left onto the lakeside road and pulled into a large vacant lot.  This was the Bus Stand. There was a small hut for an office, a few trees, a couple of small tea stalls, a few groups of would-be passengers sitting waiting in whatever shade they could find – and a collection of red and white buses in various states of disrepair.  Several of these would obviously never move again and provided a source of spare parts for cannibalization.  They belonged to the M.P. State Transport – whose dense network covered all the State, joining up major cities like Bhopal and Indore, but also remarkably remote villages.  The buses were slow, uncomfortable, often late, occasionally had to be pushed by the passengers, but they got you there in the end!

I was on my way to Jabalpur, to spend the night with the Chauhan family before going on to Bombay by train.  The bus arrived an hour late from Bhopal and got later as we went on.  We drove with all the windows open but the heat was stifling and we were covered with dust from the road.  I was glad to arrive at "Jab", take a cycle rickshaw to Wright Town, be welcomed enthusiastically by the children, "Mick, Mick, Mick!!!" and have a bath.

The Chauhan house, home to Vijay's brothers Ajay and Munna and their younger sister Mumta, was one of my several second homes in India and I often stayed there.  I particularly enjoyed playing with the children.  Kartic, the little boy on the left in the photo, still lives there with his wife and children and his mother Munni.  They welcomed me there with my wife Carole in 2012.

The Chauhans were a highly educated and political family. Vijay taught Political Science at Sagar, Ajay was Dean of Student Welfare at Jabalpur - and an *eminence* grise in State level politics - while Munna taught English in a Degree College. Their mother was the Hindi poet and freedom fighter Subhadra Kumari Chauhan[1]. Interned shortly after giving birth, she was allowed to take her baby with her, so Mumta spent the first few months of her life in a British prison cell.

On this occasion the house was – as not unusual – full. There were a couple of student friends from Sagar and cousin Dilip Chauhan, surgical registrar at one of the big Bombay hospitals

---

[1] 1904 – 1948.

with whom I had stayed the previous Christmas.  He was on his way back and we decided to travel together the next day.

That evening, we (the men that is) went to a club called the Pagoda and drank whisky paid for by Munna's friends.  I wonder if such places still exist.  We went on to the Republic Restaurant where I paid for dinner.

Next morning, I washed my clothes – remember I was travelling very light – and the children amused themselves by doing everything they could to interrupt me.

My leather camera case was coming unstitched, so we went out and found a wayside cobbler who quickly mended it for a few pice[2].  I was reminded of this in 2012 when we arrived at Kartic's with the handle of one of our suitcases broken.

"I'm going to have to buy a new case before we catch the plane back," I said.

"Don't be silly," said Kartic, calling one of his servants and sending him off into the street with my suitcase, to return half an hour later with a new handle riveted onto it.  The same make-do-and-mend mentality still existed here.  Inflation had, however, been at work in the last 45 years and pice had disappeared from circulation:

"Give him five rupees," said Kartic.

Dilip went off at lunchtime to buy tickets for the evening's Howrah-Bombay "Up" Mail.  He returned with news that there was a so-called "People's Express" at 3 p.m., a couple of hours before the Mail.  This was an unscheduled and unadvertised train.  We later learnt that it was a Pilgrim Special going back empty from Benares.

At 2 o'clock we took a cycle rickshaw to the station.  The temperature was 45°C and the streets were almost deserted.

---

[2] Decimalisation had come to India before the UK.  The centuries-old system (four paise to the anna, 16 annas to the rupee) had been replaced by 100 new pice = 1 rupee in 1957. People still often gave small prices in annas, however.

We felt sorry for the rickshaw-wallah working in this heat and gave him a big tip (big that is by Indian standards).

Trains which run two or three day routes don't stop for the heat, so the station was crowded as usual.  While we were waiting, the "Down" Mail to Howrah came in.  I had never seen a train so full, with people standing on the running boards and hanging out of the windows!  But our train came in almost empty and we easily found two berths.  The train remained almost empty all the way to Bombay.  Everyone who wanted had a berth but didn't have to pay the supplement or reservation.  There was only a skeleton staff – we didn't see a ticket collector until an hour before Bombay.  The norm on long train trips was for sweepers to pass frequently up and down with twig hand-brushes, moving the dirt around, but our coaches were never swept.  We kept expecting the Up Mail – which had priority – to overtake us, but it never did and we arrived at Bombay an hour before its scheduled arrival time.  We were in the train 24 hours.  Had we waited for the Mail, we might not have got on.

We drew into Victoria Terminus at 3 p.m. on Saturday afternoon. This enormous railway station, built in 1887 in British High Gothic style with Mughal flourishes and named to commemorate the Queen Empress's Golden Jubilee, was renamed Chhatrapati Shivaji Terminus in 1996 after the 17th century Maratha King, but everyone calls it simply "CST".  It is the only railway station I know classed as a UNESCO World Heritage Site.  The station was bustling with thousands of long-distance and commuter passengers, with red-shirted, turbaned coolies pushing luggage trollies and with chai and snack-wallahs, newspaper vendors and so on rushing from carriage to carriage.

This was my third visit to Bombay.

The first was on arrival in India the previous August when my initial reaction was shock at a level of poverty I had never encountered before.  On that occasion, together with other newly arrived volunteers, I was lodged in a Salvation Army hostel, shown the sights of Bombay from chauffeur-driven British Council cars, introduced to the British expatriate community and "briefed" at British Council headquarters about living and working in India.

The second was at Christmas after several months living up-country. This time I stayed in Dilip's room in the doctors' hostel at Bombay Hospital and spent my time with a group of young Indian doctors and their friends. Comparing now to Sagar rather than London, I found Bombay "a great modern city!" and wandering around freely with Indians saw things from a more local point of view.

This third time, I felt I was coming to a town I knew well, but I was going to see other aspects of it. I had arranged to stay a few days with an English friend, Martin Pick. I had met Martin – 22 like me and a former volunteer in Botswana – at Christmas. As a junior manager at the Bombay office of the Oxford University Press, he was provided with a company flat in the business district.

I said goodbye to Dilip and found a taxi to take me to Martin's. I arrived to be welcomed by a note saying, "Gone out for the day, make yourself at home." This I did, having a bath, changing my clothes and handing them to the children of the live-in servant family for washing, then settled down in the sitting room to catch up on the newspapers and finish a long letter home which I had started four days earlier in Sagar. I wrote:

*I am now sitting being overawed by the luxury of Martin's flat & being looked after by two little servant boys. It is much cooler here, yet one sweats more because the humidity is greater.*

I finished with references to the news and enclosed press cuttings unfortunately since lost...

*1) The article "Smear Against India" illustrates the pathological sensitivity common here (national inferiority complex – they run their country down all the time, but no-one else is allowed to criticise at all)*

*2) The cartoon & real photo of "Kutch Satyagrahis" shows politicians marching into the Kutch desert to protest against the Government's handing over of part of the Rann to Pakistan. The demonstrators wanted the Govt. to supply water in army vehicles & described the refusal as "harassment". The police cooperated at first by declaring the area as "prohibited" & thus arrested the demonstrators just inside the line. When, on some days, the police delayed their arrests & allowed the brave "men of truth & anger" to march on unhindered into the desert, this too was described as "harassment". I think these two cuttings sum it up beautifully.*

*By the way, we read a lot here at the moment about England turning into a land of race riots after the scandalous racialist speech of Enoch Powell[3]. a) is it true? & b) what exactly did Powell say? – was it so bad?*

At 10 pm Martin and his flatmate Matthew – another ex-VSO working for OUP – still hadn't come home, so I went to bed. They arrived a few minutes later and I got up again and we had a long discussion about exam corruption which seemed endemic in Indian higher education.

I stayed a week with Martin, living in expat luxury and meeting people from his overlapping circles of friends from both the international and the local artistic communities. It was Martin's declared intention to integrate as far as possible into the life of whatever country he was living in at the time, but here in Bombay, working for a major British publishing house, it was obvious that he could not avoid expatriates.

One of the first I met was a young Goan artist called Nelson – or as he preferred to write it, "Nail Sun", which allowed him to sign his pictures with a double pictogram. I found it confusing that someone from the recently annexed or liberated Portuguese colony should be named after the British naval hero!

---

[3] The infamous anti-immigration "Rivers of Blood" speech given in Birmingham 20 April 1968

He must have been about 25. He was slim, brash, self-confident, iconoclastic and amusing. He dressed sharp Western, had long black hair, moustache and pointy beard.

Nelson had invented "chipping Bombay", a variant on "bleeding Madras" – the tartan material with non-fast dies popular in the 60's. He bought shirts and jackets and decorated them with thick acrylic paint – which chipped off from wash to wash. He wore these himself and hoped he would make a fortune if and when the fashion caught on. I don't believe it ever did.

That week, the Jehangir Art Gallery – national centre for contemporary art in the Fort district – was holding an open exhibition. Nelson had the distinction of being the only artist to have his painting rejected – presumably because it was the only nude. Had it been on grounds of artistic quality half the exhibits should have been rejected. There was some extremely tatty, amateurish stuff – I can still see a pen and ink "portrait" of J. F. Kennedy clumsily copied from a photograph.

Nelson was annoyed about this and decided to demonstrate by holding a one man "preface" show outside the gallery. He nailed a tract to a tree on the pavement and propped his picture up against it. Nelson's notice reads:

> *THIS IS A PREFACE: To the Art Society of India (Golden Jubilee Exhibition) being held inside the Gallery. This painting had to remain on the pavement because the selectors SINGLED it out for rejection of all the entries*          *Nail Sun*

I was planning to stop in Goa on my way down to Kerala and Nelson advised me that the best and cheapest way to get to his home State was to travel deck class on the overnight ferry from Bombay to Panjim.

Another striking character I met was Trois Johnson, when we had lunch in his flat. Trois, a plump man of about 30, had been posted to Bombay as Medical Officer to the US Peace Corps. Trois was a humanitarian *bon vivant* and polymath. After qualifying as a doctor, he had read Sanskrit and Anthropology at Harvard and was a specialist in the history of Portuguese India. He lived in what I considered great luxury amid a fantastic collection of books, records and Indian fine art. He was to die in the Maldives in 1979 while working there for the WHO and part of his private library is preserved in the Dr. Trois Johnson Room of the Ames South Asia Library in Iowa. I found him great fun – as did the Peace Corps volunteers who kept dropping in until they filled the flat. These volunteers struck me as more impressive and open than the embattled and embittered little group I had met in Jabalpur, trying to protect themselves from all things Indian.

After lunch we drove to a big block of flats where Martin had a friend and we bathed in the swimming pool – the first I had seen, let alone entered in India; I presume someone lent me swimming trunks! Then on to the annual inaugural function of the Indian National Theatre Group. It was my introduction to Indian classical dancing, which I found hypnotic, repetitive and hard to understand. First, as at all functions, we had to sit through speeches – including that of the president – an elderly lady – on what was already becoming a familiar theme 20 years after Independence: the disintegration of national unity.

And finally to a restaurant where we ate a big meal and watched a group of American sailors singing love songs to three "old European-looking ladies".

And so the week passed with cultural activities and visiting. But also certain worries and frustrations.  One morning around 7.30 I phoned my official British Council "host family" only to be told by a sleepy voice "Mr. Howgate has returned to the UK." Then there was Terry, a "hippy character from Hull" – one of those independent young people who were travelling around Asia alone.  Somehow he turned up on Martin's doorstep one evening.  We found Terry very nice – but suffering apparently from hepatitis and we weren't sure how infectious this was, so Martin took him in, arranged for someone to take him to hospital next morning, but made him sleep out on the balcony. We were a bit shamefaced when we got the diagnosis next day – "simply suffering from exhaustion – nothing infectious!"

# 3. From Bombay to Goa

I was also trying to finalise my trip to Goa.  Dilip was going to give me the address of a friend there, but I was having trouble getting back in touch with him at the hospital.  When I phoned he was always in the theatre or at lunch!  And Nelson hadn't told me where to get my ferry ticket.  Mr. Raman at the British Council recommended a travel agent – who knew nothing about ferries but only ocean-going liners and sent me off to the tourist office, which was a bit more helpful.

I ended up at the ferry wharf in Girgaon in a long queue for tickets.  We were at the height of the Father Ferrer controversy.  Ferrer, a popular Jesuit missionary had just been served an expulsion order[4].  Political parties and newspapers had lined up on each side: pro and anti-Ferrer. As the only European in the queue, at least one of my neighbours took me for an obvious missionary:

"What are you doing here?"

"I'm trying to buy a ticket for Goa."

"Goa? Go away!  We don't want foreign missionaries here. Go back to your country!"

"But…"

"India is our country and we are proud of it!"

"Good," I said.

After an hour, I reached the head of the queue to be eyed rather quizzically by the clerk.

"You are wanting cabin? First class?"

"No, deck class."

---

[4] Vicente Ferrer (Barcelona 1920 – Anantpur A.P. 2009) – arrived in Mumbai as missionary 1952, and was expelled 1968 to enormous public protest.  Indira Gandhi allowed him to return in 1969. He left the priesthood, married, had children & continued humanitarian work amongst the poor in Andhra Pradesh until his death.

"You are aware is not very comfortable?"

"No problem!"

And I had my ticket.

I went from there to the British Council to report to the Representative, Dr. Coombs, as far as I was concerned the "big boss" in VSO's "overseas arm". We had a long chat about the nine months I had just spent in Sagar and my opinions on the posting. I then mentioned my experience in the queue at Girgaon.

"That's interesting. We've been asked to send a volunteer to Father Ferrer's project. We've been hesitating. What do you think?"

I can't remember what I thought – and didn't note it in my diary!

The next day I was back at the British Council and stumbled into a farewell reception for the outgoing British High Commissioner John Freeman, who was on his way to Washington as Ambassador. Freeman was a well-known war hero, left wing Labour politician, journalist, TV personality and diplomat. I tried to hide, but Coombs spotted me and insisted on introducing "Michael, one of our volunteers."

Freeman asked where I was off to and when I told him, turned on the "Goa" record, giving me that year's official British line on India's annexation of the Portuguese colony. I wasn't very impressed and described him as follows:

*"He's a huge man with bad teeth and a blotchy red face, amiable but overbearing and  booming out platitudes, one of those people who can just turn it on and speak about almost anything. It all seemed rather false and over self-confident."*

On Saturday 11th May, I was up at 7.00 ready to leave. I tipped Martin's servant Narayan 10 rupees. I felt this was gross extravagance but had nothing smaller and wanted to build up a favourable reputation against a possible later visit!

I was more parsimonious in the taxi to Ferry Wharf.  The driver asked for 4 Rs but quickly descended to 2.80 Rs when I protested.

There was great confusion at the Wharf with a couple of hundred people milling around giving each other contradictory advice.  Finally, we all got on the boat – a relatively small coastal steamer which reminded me of the Liverpool to Isle of Man ferries of my youth.

I was travelling by the lowest class, which cost me Rs 19.25.  This meant sleeping on the floor, but then so did upper class – at Rs 27.  Admittedly the upper had a little more room and was on a higher, more open deck, but I didn't think that justified the difference. Everyone spread out blankets or mats to sleep on – so there was quite a struggle for space.

I looked for a good place to sleep and finally found what seemed a spacious spot to spread out my yellow cotton bedspread to claim floor-space.  The deck was, of course, hard and my "bedding" very thin, but I was young and fit.  The main drawback was that I had settled in a thoroughfare, where passengers streamed back and forth, often walking on my "bed", which rapidly became filthy.

My Goan neighbours returning home were – as usual in India – friendly and interested in me, but they had some very un-Indian characteristics.  I noticed that many of them were handing round bottles of what proved to be a very potent alcoholic drink known as fenny which was distilled from cashew nuts.  This was freely and cheaply available on the boat – quite a change from "dry" Bombay! They shared it with me instead of the usual sweets or chapattis and I found it very agreeable.  As the day went on, some of my fellow passengers even got drunk and started falling about.

The Goans spoke what seemed to me a strange mixture of Portuguese and Hindi, but some of them also had some English and we managed to communicate.

We cast off at 11 a.m. and sailed south down the coast for ten hours.  About 9 p.m. we hove to off a large headland, with a lighthouse and a small town with its lights twinkling in the bay. Here we dropped anchor and I went up on deck just in time to see three boats packed with passengers and freight looming out of the darkness, propelled by energetic oarsmen standing in the bows.

We arrived at Panjim, since officially renamed Panaji, capital of the State of Goa, at eight o'clock on Sunday morning, sailed through a narrow channel into the natural harbour of the Mandovi River estuary and tied up in the waterfront main street. I had taken up my bed like Lazarus and was waiting rather bleary-eyed in the morning sunshine with the crowd impatient to get off.

I was keen to see this atypical part of India, which had been "Portuguese" much longer than the rest had been "British".

Vasco da Gama had opened the sea route from Europe to India in 1497, five years after Columbus "discovered" America. The Portuguese had conquered Goa, a province of the Bijapur Sultanate, in 1510, establishing their capital in the Sultan's provincial capital of Velha (old) Goa on the banks of the Mandovi, about 15 km upriver from present day Panaji. The Portuguese ruled Goa for 450 years – for much of this time as an overseas province.  In comparison, the British East India Company, only set up its first trading stations in 1612, and started acquiring sovereignty, gradually shared with the British Crown, in 1757.  The British Raj as such, with Queen Victoria as its first Empress, was only set up in 1858 after the ill-fated First War of Independence - still referred to as the "Indian Mutiny" in the history books I studied at school.

British rule lasted until 1947, when Churchill and Mountbatten partitioned the sub-continent along majority religious lines, signing Hindu "India" away to Jawaharlal Nehru and Muslim "Pakistan" to Mohammed Ali Jinnah.  The Indian Government made the not unreasonable request that Portugal should hand over its relatively tiny enclave at the same time. The Portuguese didn't see things that way and hung on until 1961, when Nehru – known for his pacifism – lost patience and sent troops in despite international controversy. The Indian attack was codenamed "Operation Vijay" (Victory) and this proved to be an accurate name. The Portuguese dictator Salazar called on his troops to fight to the last man and die rather than surrender, but the battle in fact lasted only two days with a couple of dozen fatalities on each side.

When I visited, Goa was a centrally administered Union territory, which it remained until 1987. It is now the smallest and one of the richest fully-fledged States of the Indian Union.

After 450 years of direct rule, I expected Goa to be much more "European" than most of India. My first impressions confirmed this. On the boat, I had already been struck by the liberal attitude to alcohol, and my first sight of Goan architecture made me think I had landed in a small Spanish seaside town. It was obvious from the complexions around me that there had been much more intermarriage in Goa than in the India I knew.

But my first priority was to find a place to stay! Back in Bombay, I had finally reconnected with Dilip Chauhan, we had met for a meal and he had given me my unsuspecting host's office phone number. His friend Paddu was a researcher at the National Institute of Oceanography. All I had to do was find him. Unfortunately, Dilip didn't have his home address.

Once on dry land, surrounded by noisy family reunions, I asked directions and walked to the Post Office to telephone. I asked the telephone clerk to connect me to the Institute. After letting it ring for some time, he looked up at me.

"I am sorry, sir. Nobody is answering. Is Sunday morning. Offices are closed."

I was at a bit of a loss what to do next, but a friendly postman told me that two of "the Doctors" lived in a flat over their workplace 4 km away at Miramar and that I would surely find them there, so I took a taxi and was overcharged by the driver – who was deeply insulted when I challenged him.

"We are reasonable here, Sir!"

He left me at an unprepossessing two storey concrete building near the beach.  I knocked at all the doors I could find, but the place was deserted except for a young man taking a shower outside behind the building.  I assumed he must be the watchman and when I asked for information he assured me:

"Dr. Chandra Shekar will surely be coming here at 11.30, Sir."

I hoped he was right, as it was now past 9 o'clock and the sun was getting steadily hotter.  There wasn't much else I could do, so I sat on the Institute wall with my small metal suitcase on my knees, took out an aerogramme form and using the case as a writing desk, started writing a letter home:

*Dear Mum & Dad,*
*Well, here I am in Goa.  It's 10 o'clock in the morning and I'm sitting on the wall of the Institute of Oceanography waiting for someone to turn up …*

The setting was idyllic – my first experience of the tropical South Indian countryside.  I was surrounded by coconut palms and a pleasant breeze was blowing in from the sea at my back. A little further off were a few huts thatched with palm fronds where a group of young children were dragging animals about – mainly dogs and goats. The birds were still singing despite the heat, though they were keeping out of the direct sun with the exception of swallows which kept swooping across my field of vision.  Big lizards, maybe 25 cm long, were running up and down the palm trees and I was impressed by the size of the butterflies.

I was beginning to get nervous – and very hungry – when a sort of minibus jeep came bounding down the road with three jolly, youngish men in it and drew up noisily in front of this strange young European sitting on their wall.

It turned out to be the purest chance that they were passing that way on Sunday morning, but they were happy to see me and drove me up the hill to Paddu's house for breakfast.

Paddu and his two colleagues, Shekar and Shrivastava, were the core research staff of the tiny Institute set up two years earlier in the rented building where I had been waiting. This has since grown into a major international research centre with over 300 staff.  All three had "been out", in other words had studied abroad, one in Canada, one in Germany, one in Russia.  I would later meet their director, Dr Setty.  None of these people were native Goans:  they were Indian Civil Servants and the setting up of the new National Institute could be considered as part of the Union Government's policy of integrating this newly annexed territory.  Though I met native Goans during my stay, I would actually spend most of my time with expatriate middle class Indians!  My view of Goan life was therefore doubly external.

At breakfast, I was introduced to Paddu's young wife Maya

who was expecting their first child.  I discovered that she was sister to Munni, Munna Chauhan's wife back in Jabalpur. Small world! I would meet her again 45 years later in Jabalpur, a widow who happened to be staying with Munni – also widowed – and her son Kartic when my wife and I called on them in 2012.

After a siesta we drove down to Miramar Beach.  This small town had a very Iberian air – result of centuries of Portuguese rule.  Then on across the headland to the jetty at Dona Paula – another typically Portuguese place name -  where I watched Paddu set up an experiment – submerging small bottles in the sea.  Across the bay, we could see Goa's biggest city – the international port of Vasco da Gama – proudly named after the 15th century navigator.  For the next 24 hours Paddu would drive back every three hours to take measurements.

I had been in India nine months now and had frequently been welcomed into peoples' homes in major cities or remote villages.  But I had always – at least on my first visit – been accompanied, taken home by someone to meet their family and friends.  This was the first time I had turned up somewhere alone, unknown and unexpected.  I don't think I even had a note of introduction, just Paddu's name and the phone number of the Institute on a scrap of paper with the oral instruction "tell him you're a friend of Dilip's and the Jabalpur Chauhans."

I was welcomed as an old friend or a member of the family – and I stayed a week.  During this time not only Paddu and his wife, but also his colleagues at the Institute modified their timetables to make sure I had an interesting time.  Sometimes I accompanied them and watched them at work, sometimes they took time off and borrowed official vehicles to show me around, sometimes they put me into a bus with detailed instructions of where I should get off and what I was going to see.  In the evenings I accompanied Paddu on his scooter to play badminton, to get my hair cut or to drink in a bar.  Much of one such evening was spent repairing both tyres of the said scooter, which had managed to find nails on the road home.

One day, we had a trip down through the lush countryside to the Southern city of Margoa.  This was meant as a day out for us boys, but was officially billed as driving practice for two of the staff.  Unfortunately, the Institute Director got wind of the scheme, but to my surprise, instead of banning it, decided to come along and bring his wife and little daughter for the ride.  This rather spoilt the atmosphere – particularly as the little girl refused to eat in the restaurant and threw a tantrum which lasted nearly an hour.  We left the restaurant and drove through the town with all the passers by turning to see where the screaming was coming from.  The parents had absolutely no control:

"We don't <u>know</u> what to do with her – her grandmother has spoiled her."

Another day, we were sitting in the Institute when a couple of peasants came over from the nearby huts.  They shinned up a couple of the nearer palm trees with their feet in loops of rope around the trunk.  At the top, they took cutlasses from their belts and started lopping down fronds and bunches of coconuts.  When they came down we asked for a couple of nuts.  These they gave us – cutting them open with their cutlasses.  We offered to pay, but they just laughed and refused.  They were full of juice and flesh – delicious – very different from the nuts I was used to eating back home dried-out after weeks in a ship's hold.

As in southern Europe, Catholicism was a major influence in Goa.  I have said it was easy to believe one was in a town in the South of Spain and my clearest memory is of the numerous Catholic churches - in particular the monumental Immaculate Conception Church in downtown Panaji with its zigzagging staircases up to the main doors. My visit coincided with the festival of Our Lady of Fatima – and I saw several processions of Catholic faithful.  Though Christians are a tiny minority in India as a whole, they – mainly Catholics - represented over a third of the Goan population in 1968, largely I believe in the educated, urban populations.  A corollary of this was the large Goan influence on the Catholic church in India as a whole.  I had had personal experience of this the year before, after four days in the country, when the first Indian to invite me into his home turned out to be a Goan: the Archbishop of Bhopal, Eugene D'Souza – met in the train North from Bombay to Sagar.

**Immaculate Conception Church**

It was in Goa that St. Francis Xavier, co-founder of the Jesuit order and Papal Nuncio to the Far East, started his mission to convert Asia to Christianity in 1542. After his death in China in 1552, his body was shipped back to Goa, where it is enshrined in a massive glass and silver sarcophagus in the Baroque Bom Jesus Basilica in Old Goa. I visited this with a tourist bus full of Goan pilgrims. They explained to me that the Saint's body used to be exhibited openly, but that his toes were beginning to corrupt from too much kissing by pilgrims, so he had been sealed into the glass case for protection. I'm not sure how accurate this was, as Wikipedia tells me the glass case dates back to 1637.

There were, of course, Hindu temples, many of them influenced by Iberian ecclesiastical architecture and looking rather like churches or monasteries. Unlike my experiences in Northern India, I was refused entrance to these as an obvious non-Hindu. Was this a result of the historic dominance of

Catholicism? The priests at the door were polite, but firm – and spoke excellent English.

**Hindu temple, Old Goa**

Goa is also known for its fine beaches.  My Indian hosts told me stories of the" invasion" by Western hippies, who dressed and behaved in a scandalous manner.  Perhaps I went to the wrong beaches, but those I saw were more or less deserted except for a few Indians who were behaving most decorously – none even trying to swim, but quite a few sitting fully clothed in the water.

On the Saturday, Paddu's sister and deaf old father turned up unexpectedly from Jabalpur, as one did in those days, with a couple of heavy trunks and bulky bedrolls.  They were bringing presents – mostly little girls' frocks – for the imminently expected baby.  I wondered how they were so sure it was a girl.  This was before the days of echography, so I can only presume they had consulted an astrologer!

I had really settled into this little family microcosm in Panjim, but I decided it was time for me to move on.  After all, my students expected me in Kerala "anytime from the 15th".  It was already the 18th and Kerala still several days' journey away.

I was also beginning to think that with my small suitcase and haversack I was "travelling heavy".  Here was an opportunity to lighten my load by sending a few things back to Jabalpur in the new guests' trunks.  I could always retrieve them a couple of months later.

My journey from Goa to Kerala by bus and train would take me five days.  I would cross the State of Mysore[5], roughly the size of England and Scotland, from North to South, cross briefly

---

[5] Renamed Karnataka in 1973

into Madras State[6], climb from sea level to 2,200m and back, all this while trying to learn something of the complex Dravidian culture, architecture and history with their Mughal and British colonial overlays.

Paddu told me I must see Bangalore, Mysore and the Nilgiri hill stations and he gave me a note of introduction to his friend "Clod" in Mysore – together with two bottles of cashew fenny – one as a farewell gift to me, the other as a present for his friend. These I carefully stowed in my haversack.

------

[6] Modern Tamilnadu

# 4. On to Bangalore

Once again I abandoned a newly found comfort zone and prepared to head into the unknown. I had an 800 km bus journey ahead of me, with changes in Hubli and Bangalore. Apparently there was a system of seat reservation here in the South – something unheard of in Madhya Pradesh – and my hosts considered it essential for me to use it, so there was a great rush on Sunday morning to get me to the bus stand in time to do so.  They needn't have bothered:

"I am sorry, sir, there is no reservation service on Sundays."

We were early and the bus was late and quite full, but there was no problem getting on.  It was a "luxury" service – which basically meant the seats had headrests and the passengers were middle class.

While waiting, I was accosted by the only other European in the bus station. Fred was a rather dour German traveller about my age who was scruffily dressed and stank to high heaven as his shirt and trousers had obviously not been washed for days and nor had he. This really marked him out amongst the Goans and other Indian passengers – all simply dressed but spotless and well-starched, sweet-smelling and obviously freshly bathed – as in fact was I.   Fred explained with pride that his negative hygiene was a deliberate ploy.  He was on his way to Madras to catch a boat to Thailand. He had been informed that as a European he would be obliged to hire a cabin.  To avoid this additional expense and qualify to travel deck class, he was working to become as disreputable as possible.  He proposed that we travel together as far as Bangalore, where our routes diverged.  With mixed feelings, I agreed.

Fred grumbled a lot – the bus was late, he found this typical. Indians weren't very friendly: on the one hand they tried to cheat him out of his money, on the other they seemed to look down on him.  Perhaps I should have tried to persuade him that his own behaviour had something to do with this, but I didn't bother.  In Frankfurt or Wiesbaden, he would have been avoided as a down and out – why expect better treatment in India? He wasn't much of a conversationalist, but luckily there were a couple of young students sitting nearby who struck up a conversation – with me not Fred!

Early in our journey, I was discussing the weather with one of these young men. It looked very much like rain: clouds were building up, there was thunder and lightning.  Suddenly, I felt drips – it was raining inside the bus!  But what was that smell?  I looked up and saw my haversack leaking – my bottle of cashew fenny had cracked and soaked into my bedding.  I got the haversack down and took out the bottle. The driver saw this in his mirror and turned round to wave angrily at me:

"Sir, no sir!  No drinking alcoholic drinks on bus!  Put bottle away!"

From then until the next bath, I too had a strong smell.

Our route took us up the Western Ghats at dusk – an unforgettable view as the narrow road wound up and up through the forest, which opened out every few hundred metres into a sudden panorama – miles and miles of hills rolling down to a thin strip of golden sea.

After an extremely uncomfortable night in our "luxury" bus, we arrived about 7.30 at Bangalore.  I was hoping to stay with a VSO called John Martin, but attempts to contact him by phone failed.  So Fred and I explored the streets around the bus stand, fighting off touts and coolies:

"You want nice hotel, two rupees?"

"You looking for girls?"

After half an hour we checked in to an un-inviting but fairly respectable looking Indian style hotel (this meant you had a bed, but supplied your own bedding), the Janpath, where we paid 10 rupees for a twin bedded room.  We had a short nap, I washed the fenny out of my bedding and haversack then had a shower (but Fred didn't – he had a project!).   Then we set out to explore, closing the room with the padlock from my suitcase.

My memory of pre-computer Bangalore is fairly vague.  I remember a spacious, open city with wide streets and interesting monuments.   We visited Tipu Sultan's Summer Palace with its carved and gilded wooden colonnades on two levels.  The building was absolutely deserted when we visited, the effect rich but remarkably cosy – the arches being approximately my height.

By contacting missionaries at Trinity Church, I finally ran John Martin to ground – a cheerful Liverpudlian from Flint, about to return home after a year boring wells with Afpro (Action for Food Production) – an NGO still very active in 21$^{st}$ century India[7]. I considered – still do – that what he was doing was considerably more useful than my English Literature teaching!

The three of us went to the cinema that evening and watched the 1965 film of *Lord Jim* starring Peter O'Toole.  I

---

[7] www.afpro.org

found the film's ambiguous "white man's burden" theme rather upsetting.  God knows what the Indian audience made of it!

I spent a disturbed night at the Janpath, what with Fred's smell and snoring, frequent wakenings imagining I was being bitten by non-existent bedbugs and an attack of hay fever in the early hours.

Fred slipped away about 6.30 and I left a little later to seek out the bus for Mysore.

May '68! I bought a copy of the Hindustan Times to read on this 4-hour journey.  Once settled in my seat, I unfolded it and was amazed to read of rioting in Paris and see photos of street fighting between students and gendarmes.  What was France coming to?

Once in a bus or train, I felt safe and part of me wished the journey would never end.  If there were friendly English-speaking passengers, we would chat.  If not, I would watch the countryside and read.  As we neared the next destination, however, anxiety would mount: I had to take my destiny in hand again, find my directions, find someone helpful who spoke English.  Where would I sleep that night?  Usually things worked out well.

I got down from the bus at Mysore and somehow found myself on the right local bus to Clod's house on the outskirts of the city.

"Clod" turned out to be Claude, scion of a Catholic family with some French connection.  He was another of the larger-than-life characters I kept bumping into in India.  Advocate at the local court, he also kept European breeds of cows and pigs at the bottom of his garden and supplied pork to the local food research institute.  Surprised to see me, he was very welcoming and plied me with rum.  His 12-year old nephew Vivekund was staying with him – an old-fashioned but vivacious little boy who was afraid of the dark.  Vivvy, as we called him, was nominated to be my tourist guide for the next day.

**Seringapatam – Vivvy and Juggernaut**

Wednesday was a day of exhaustive – and exhausting – tourism.  With my young guide, I visited Mysore town itself and also Tipu Sultan's fabulous walled city of Seringapatam.  I found the relationship with Vivvy difficult.  I wasn't used to dealing with small boys and it wasn't clear If I was taking him out, or he was taking me.  We had constant disagreements – he seemed always worried and never satisfied.  I think I also overestimated his physical abilities.  A great walker at the time, I learned some weeks later by roundabout channels that I had been considered mean for making him walk in the heat rather than taking rickshaws and taxis...

We got back to Claude's by the last bus, after 9 p.m. to find an unannounced family gathering.  One of Claude's brothers had arrived by car from Bombay with his wife and children.  We sat down to eat, with the rum flowing freely for the men.

The brother became a little drunk and started running down 'the so-called British' he had met, and their hospitality, claiming, 'They still think we're just a bunch of niggers.'

As the only "so-called British" in the room, I couldn't help feeling targeted, even though he kept turning to me and prefacing his remarks with, "I don't know about you, don't know what you think, don't even know your name, but..."

Claude had also served me quite a bit of rum, which fuelled my resentment at being held responsible both for the exactions of the British Raj and for lingering post-colonial racism.  My hosts tried to shut the brother up, but he wouldn't drop the subject, so, tired and a little drunk as I was, I finally snapped, stood up for myself and we had quite a nasty exchange in which I traded stereotype for stereotype and expressed myself on the less lovable character traits of certain Indians – present company not excepted.  Later his wife and mother came and apologized for him, but I went to bed ashamed and unhappy.

In the morning, my host was rather distant – but the brother was very friendly and cheerful, showed no hard feelings and insisted on lending his car to take me to the bus station.  I was on my way to visit Ooty – the Nilgiri hill station which had been the Summer Capital of the British Madras Presidency.

"You must eat at my friend's hotel beside the race course," said Claude.  "The food is excellent and if you tell him Claude sent you, he will give you a big reduction on the price."

It was a long uncomfortable journey, climbing 2,000 metres on narrow, winding mountain roads, though the scenery was beautiful and at the top there was a delightful cool breeze.  I was feeling guilty and unhappy about the previous evening and feeling lonely.

Halfway up from the plain, we stopped in a village where the road dipped down to cross a small river.  There was much excitement, and villagers were streaming down the road in front of us as if for a Sunday outing.  We were told the road was blocked by a tree a little further on.  Our driver preferred to wait in the village, but some of us got down to see what was happening.  We walked about a mile and came to a mass of cars and buses.  A huge banyan tree had collapsed across the road where it crossed the stream.  One bus had tried to drive round the obstacle and had got stuck in the river.  The villagers were doing a fine job chopping away with axes and machetes and we - bus passengers – helped by dragging the great boughs out of the way.  After about an hour the road was clear, the traffic jam started to ease and our bus came down the road and picked us up.

I saw little of Ooty and wasn't very impressed with what I saw.  The feeling I had was of a rather dilapidated English market town – Newmarket comes to mind.  I dined at the hotel of Claude's friend – who gave me a princely 10% discount on a very ordinary meal.  I watched the horses exercising on the race course and decided not to spend the night here, but to press on (i.e. back down) to Coimbatore.

I should have taken the picturesque Nilgiri Mountain Railway. This 19th century narrow gauge rack and pinion railway which winds through the Blue Mountains has since been classed as a UNESCO world heritage site – but it was and is very slow. I was feeling unadventurous, tired and depressed and decided to take the much faster bus.  Faster and more modern – but the passengers still had to push the bus to start it!

At Coimbatore I went to the station, bought my ticket to Ernakulum and telegraphed ahead to announce my arrival, then found a tolerably respectable but shabby small hotel and asked to be woken at 6 am.  I found there was no way of locking the bedroom door, so pushed the bed up against it.

# 5. Arrival in Kerala

*A cleaner, greener land!*
Rudyard Kipling, *Mandalay*

The hotel boy woke me at 4.30 instead of 6, so I was in plenty of time for the Cochin Mail.

It was a four or five-hour journey and I had a reservation in the 2-tier coach. Unfortunately, I was opposite a very sick old man, whose son was apparently taking him either to or from hospital. The poor man was very thin and kept puking into a vile smelling handkerchief. This was very unpleasant for those of us in close proximity to him. He reminded me of my Gran, whom I had watched dying of cancer for several weeks at home in Liverpool when I was 13. I thought at the time that it would be nice if Indian Railways allowed such people a first-class compartment at third class fare – if only for the sake of the other passengers. Luckily he soon reached his destination and his son gently helped him out of the train.

I was then befriended by a ticket collector called Prabhu who showed great interest in me, warned me about possible confusion between the different stations at Ernakulum and even went so far as to buy me breakfast.

As we pulled into Ernakulum Town, its platforms overhung with tropical greenery, I spotted my student from Sagar, Hermachandra, running alongside the train. He banged on my window and shouted:

"Please don't get down here, sir. Get down at next station!"

He got into the compartment with me, and we went on to the larger Junction station, where Mathew John was waiting for us.

After lunch at the station, the three of us rode off on hired bicycles to the old town of Cochin with its lagoon and port. I was immediately struck by the fact that almost all the men – whatever their age or social status - wore the traditional white lungi and a Western style white short-sleeve shirt.  It was the same wherever we went in Kerala, in distinct contrast to my experience in the North where most urban men, particularly the young, dressed Western in public.  Those who didn't were usually making a cultural or even political point.   My student friend Mathew in his neat shirt and trousers was completely normal for Sagar, but stood out as exceptional in his own country! Another general impression was that everything was neater and cleaner here than in the North.

Cochin was a melting pot of cultures.  As a major port on the Malabar Coast, it had been the centre of the Spice trade for centuries, trading with the Greeks and Romans, with pre-Islamic Arabia and with China.  Legend has it that the "black" or Malabar Jewish community dates back to the destruction of the Temple in Jerusalem in 70 AD, or even to the days of King Solomon.  A second wave of European or "white" Jews, banished from Spain in 1492, found their way here in the 16th century. St. Thomas the Apostle is said to have introduced Christianity in the first century.

Catholicism arrived with the Portuguese in 1503, Protestantism with the conquering Dutch in 1663 and Anglicanism with the British in the 19th century.  For much of the 18th and 19th centuries, Kerala was part of the Muslim Mysore Sultanate.

On this first afternoon, we visited the old Jewish town – which reminded me of some medieval central European city, with its 400-year-old synagogue and its "white Jewish" community. We saw several white Jews, including "one incredibly thin old man," as I wrote at the time.

Mathew John, Hermachandra and bicycles in Jewish Town

Close by was St Francis church – known as the oldest Christian church in India. Originally built by the Portuguese and burial place of Vasco da Gama for several years before his body was shipped home to Lisbon, it later passed into Protestant Dutch and later Anglican  hands.  We were shown the old registers of births and deaths in Dutch and English – and the old cooling system – still in use – with heavy wood and cloth punkahs or flat fans, pulled by ropes from outside the church.

And so on to Mathew's home by bus.  He warned me, "Our facilities are very limited," but I found the house very pleasant – small but neat and tidy and very practical.  It was a standard "C-type" bungalow in the FACT Township, the housing development built specifically for employees of the nationalized Fertilizers and Chemicals Travancore Ltd.  Identical bungalows with small gardens, occupied by families of similar middle-management status, lined the narrow street, which was on a gentle slope.

The Johns were Plymouth Brethren, but far from the dour types often suggested by that name.  Religion was important to them: there was grace before meals and short family evening prayers, but the general atmosphere was joyful and friendly.  I didn't flaunt my agnosticism, but when asked, said I was brought up Church of England - Anglican by caste!

The evening meal was quite amusing – Mrs John had prepared small fish with hard bones and we all had difficulty removing these.  We were of course already eating in the southern fashion with neither cutlery nor chapattis. We used our fingers directly, mixing sauce, vegetables and other ingredients to form balls of rice which we could then flick into our mouths.  The additional difficulty posed by the fishbones meant that all attempts at polite table manners were abandoned!

I went to bed exhausted straight after the meal – I had after all done and seen quite a lot since being roused by the hotel boy in Coimbatore at 4.30.

Next morning, Saturday, I was taken by boat, bus and taxi to the village of Ezhikkara, where Mathew's father was born.  We spent a wonderful day boating on the lake in a traditional old canoe, powered by a single boatman with a paddle in the stern. A timeless day drifting from hamlet to hamlet between the blue sky and the green water.  I was so impressed by this new world that I used up maybe a third of a roll of my precious colour film recording it.

We often passed canoes like our own – some with straw hatted fishermen, others overloaded with passengers – all dressed in white and some carrying umbrellas against the sun. At times, I was afraid the narrow flat-bottomed boat would capsize as Mathew's friend Johnny had great fun rocking it.

All around us was a dense forest of palm trees, interspersed with huge spidery cantilevered fishing nets made from bamboo lashed together with rope and occasional palm-frond latrines overhanging the water.

**Lakeside hamlet**

Wherever we stopped, we were besieged by excited children asking, "Take my picture, take my picture!" and we were plied with food – pineapple, jackfruit... and tapioca, which though presumably nourishing is not very tasty raw!

**Cantilever fishing net**

We returned to the village for a late lunch with one of Mathew's relatives and were sitting eating on his veranda when

I noticed we were being watched from a distance by a suspicious, unfriendly looking man.

"Who's he?" I asked.

"Oh, don't take any notice of him.  That's the local Communist Party organizer.  We call him 'Bulganin'.  He probably thinks you're an American spy!"

The village was between the lake and the sea and specialized in a variety of rice which prospered in brackish water. Whenever there was a high tidal coefficient, the paddy fields would flood from the sea.  Not only, did this irrigate the fields – but it supplied a source of protein in the fish and prawns which were stranded and could be collected by hand once the water receded.

**Salt-water paddy fields**

And so back to Ernakulum by the last bus.

## 6. Elephant Hunt

Mathew John had promised me, "You will surely mount on an elephant."

Next morning, we rose at 6.0, and Mr. Varghese, an evangelist friend who was going to guide us into the interior arrived about 7.0. He was a smiling man in his forties, hair cut short and neatly parted, wearing black sandals, white short sleeved shirt and lungi folded jauntily above the knees – and carrying a black umbrella which wouldn't have been out of place in the Strand. I remember him as plump, but he would not be considered so in our days of generalized obesity.

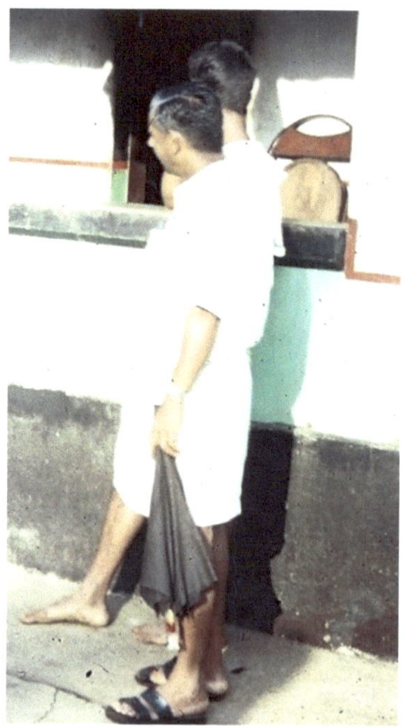

**Mr. Varghese**

He was taking us to the State Forestry Department's Elephant Training Centre in the forest behind the 210-metre-long irrigation barrage which had been completed only the year before across the Periyar River.  It was a tremendous journey, probably only 50 km but we had to take 4 buses. There was beautiful scenery, but as yet very little water in the dam, so we were allowed to walk along the bottom of the barrage below the sluices.

We crossed over and pushed through narrow jungle paths upriver to the much older "Devil's Dam".  It is said demons started this natural dam with huge slabs of rock in an attempt to flood a nearby Shiva temple, but were prevented by the rising sun from completing it, leaving a narrow gap. Here I was persuaded to shed my sandals & leap precariously from one hot boulder to another.  In the process I became a dripping rag as it was now midday, but the others, knowing how to pace themselves, remained cool and un-sweaty.

We took an extremely spicy lunch off plantain leaves in a scruffy wayside cafe.  Then as it was late, we went direct to the forestry department's training centre.  In a clearing we found two huge wooden cages built of tree trunks. Each had six elephant-sized compartments or cells – all disappointingly empty.

The director came out of his office to welcome us and explained that there would be no elephants for two years:

"There's no demand these days – tractors and trucks are cheaper to run."

So we decided to stop over in the country at Mr Varghese's house which was nearby and go to see a privately owned elephant in the morning.

Unluckily we were caught by torrential rain, and after wading through pools and crossing exposed paddy fields, we cut short our journey and took shelter, absolutely soaked, in Mr. Varghese's father's house.  I was pretty miserable, feeling sure I had caught cold, but while an attempt was made to dry our wet clothes, I learnt to put on a dhoti in the South Indian fashion – i.e. like a full length skirt. Before retiring we had a little prayer service in Malayalam, which made me uncomfortable, not knowing where and whether to say Amen.

We slept on rush mats on the floor and I was embarrassed in the morning to find my lungi had come undone – exposing all I had to all and sundry.

**Kerala style lungi**

We rose at dawn, again with prayers and set out unbathed and fasting to seek the elephant. The rain had stopped, but my clothes were still very damp. First we walked half a mile to Mr. Varghese's own small thatched house on the hillside, which we had failed to reach in the downpour the night before.  Here we cleaned our mouths and drank tea.

After further walking, we came to a large wooden house with a terrace.  Mr Varghese introduced us to the Christian family who lived there and they insisted on serving us breakfast before taking us to see their elephant.

"Babu" was standing chained up behind the house. He was only a youngster – five and a half years old, about two metres high.  His trainer Viswanathan was also a youngster –

only 21, although he'd been in the business 9 years.  This was his sixth elephant, but the first he had trained completely by himself.  During the process, his arm had been broken.

I was introduced to Babu – encouraged to stroke him and given a large chunk of jackfruit to present.  This was taken in like wood to a pulping mill.  Then I sat on him for a couple of posed photos.

Babu was apparently a beautiful specimen – correct proportions, healthy, good-tempered and a bargain at Rs 1,500 when they bought him untrained at four and a half years old (usual price 5,000 – 10,000, but the market was collapsing).  Viswanathan was also willing to work for small money to stay with this animal of which he was enormously proud and with whom he had a real complicity.  He was paid Rs 120 a month plus 10 rupees a day and all found (usual rate 25/-) when the elephant was working in the forest.

**Intrepid Brit with Babu and Vishvanathan**

Only the fairly rich could afford to keep elephants. Normally an elephant needed two men to care for it, but

Vishvanathan's junior had left a short time before.  They eat a lot too – mainly plantain leaves and other greenery but they were also occasionally given rice and meat.

"If they are needing a tonic the mahouts are also giving them chicken and goat."

"But aren't elephants vegetarian?"

"Naturally, yes, but we are dishonest!  We are having to fool them!  They are mashing up the meat and mixing it with rice into big balls – then Pop! Into elephant's mouth!"

Well, I had my ride – about two kilometres, down towards the river where the elephants were washed daily.  I rode solo and caused quite a sensation in the villages and country lanes.  An elephant is much wider than a horse – and the shoulders sway up and down as it plods along, so balance is quite tricky.  I held on most of the time to the rope round its neck which was being used for stirrups.  I found out that none of my hosts had ever ridden, and most Indians are afraid to go too near.

"You are very brave, Mr. Howarth," said Mathew.

"Why?  Haven't you ridden an elephant?"

"No, never!  None of us have.  It's too dangerous, but the trainer says the elephant likes you.  This is the first time it has allowed anyone else but him to ride.  He says he can make a trainer of you in twelve months!"

Vishvanathan rode much more stylishly than me – using no hands and commanding the elephant by kicking it gently behind the ears. I was told it also responded to about 200 different vocal commands.

**"Look, no hands!"**

We watched Babu and another larger elephant start their baths. They lay down on their sides in the shallows & Vishvanathan and two older men scrubbed away with coconut shells.

As they worked, they talked – and the discussion gradually became quite heated. The older trainers of the larger elephant seemed to be telling Vishvanathan off.

"What's the matter?" I asked.

It was Mr Varghese who replied.

"It seems there is an elephant nearby who has become disobedient. The young man has said he will go and visit this elephant this afternoon. He thinks he will be able to improve its behaviour. The others are trying to persuade him not to go. They say it is very dangerous – that there have been several fatalities in such cases – but he is young and fearless and doesn't want to listen!"

Did they persuade him? Did he go? Did he tame the recalcitrant beast? Or did it trample him to death? It would have been interesting to stay and find out, but it was time for us to start making our complicated way back to Ernakulum, so we said goodbye to the villagers and headed for the nearest bus stop.

After five days with the Evangelist Johns, it was time for me to move on.  Following an exchange of telegrams putting off my planned departure, my Muslim student Shibili was now expecting me further South.

We had a very touching parting.  I had been made to feel a real member of the family, and Mathew had gone to great trouble to arrange a programme for me.  Mr John told me he loved me as his son and had been praying for me ever since I had arrived.  He made a rapid attempt to convert me:

"I don't want to see you damned!"

And he presented me with a New Testament.

In town, I bought an umbrella and a roll of film to replace the one I had used up – black and white the only thing available – and took the noon bus to Quilon.

# 7. Shibili and co.

We rolled along 140 kilometres of beautiful coast road: this was the tropical paradise I had always imagined!  On my left the luxuriance of palm forest and backwaters, to my right coves and sandy beaches where fishermen were preparing their nets.  And everywhere small settlements along the road.  The half-way point was Alleppey – dubbed "the Venice of the East" by the imperious British Viceroy, Lord Curzon on a state visit in 1900. From here on south, the typical architecture changed, taking on what I considered a "Buddhist" form in wood and thatch (see sketch from diary). 

Shibili was waiting at the bus stand in Quilon with Baluchadran – Balu for short – another of my students from Sagar – this one Hindu.  They had been waiting some time, had already met a couple of buses and were beginning to think that I wasn't coming today either.  These were the students I had been warned against in the North as being completely untrustworthy.

I was already used to Malayalam-speaking students who came North to study.  At Quilon I discovered that Hindi-speaking beggars apparently made the opposite voyage.  We were besieged by a group of the latter:

"Give me eight annas, sahib.  Dos paisa dedo!"

We pushed our way through and went into the railway station.  We had a 20-minute journey by metre gauge train which felt more like a bus.  A little girl with a shaven head was sitting on the bunk opposite watching me, and a talkative old man struck up a conversation:

"Where are you going?"

"Varkala"

"Ah yes, Varkala.  You must be going to the sanatorium.  You must be very careful!"

"Why?"

"You mustn't touch the native liquor.  If you do, you will lose consciousness and your valuables will be stolen!"

Varkala was a little town with a disproportionate number of taxis waiting at the station.  We took one of these out to Shibili's – a nice little modern house with a tiled roof (rather than the usual thatch) right out in the country. The situation was very peaceful and we could hear the sea breaking on the beach a few hundred metres away.  The house had a very deep well and – very rare in the country – a toilet with a septic tank.  Shibili's father spoke no English, but made up for this by smiling a lot.

There was quite a little community of Sagar students in and around Varkala and they were determined to show me their version of "the real India".  They would tire me out doing so!

The first morning, we were served a large traditional Kerala breakfast of cooked plantain and "put" – steamed rolls made from rice flour and coconut, while a taxi waited to take us to Balu's house in town.  There we were obliged to eat a second breakfast before setting off on foot through narrow lanes to pick up other friends.  Finally, a cheerful group of seven or eight boys, Muslims, Hindus and me, arrived at the Hindu Shri Narayanra Ashram.  Here I was presented to the swami – a nice old man, who gave me a book in English about the founder of his sect.  We then climbed the flights of steps to the Memorial Temple on the hilltop overlooking Varkala.  My students remained cool and fresh in their lungis, but I was beginning to get very hot and sweaty in my narrow terylene trousers.  The view, however, was worth the discomfort.

We walked on and came to the small philosophy school run by Swami Nitya Chaitanya Yati.  I was often introduced to holy men in India.  In my time at least, such seers were very accessible and it was difficult for me to know if the person receiving me was "just" some local priest, or a spiritual leader of national or international renown.  Swami Nitya Chaitanya Yati was one of the latter – a philosopher who, (as I read now on http://www.in.com) published over 120 books in Malayalam and 80 in English before his death in 1999. He was particularly known for promoting the concept of World Citizenship.  When I met him in 1968, he must have been about 45, long haired and bearded, wearing typical robes.  He welcomed our oecumenical group, performed a mini-initiation, discovering an individual "Om" mantra for each of us, then served us tea and mango.  I wrote in my diary that he was leading a very comfortable life of renunciation and that he seemed very nice!

We walked back into town for a big lunch at Balu's house, then all lay down for an afternoon nap.  In the evening we walked down to the beach where the boys were proud to inform me that scenes of the current Bollywood blockbuster *Aadmi* had been filmed a few months earlier.

Mohamed Shibili (L), Balu (R) and friends on beach

On the way back to town we came to a mineral spring whose waters were said to have medicinal properties, so we all drank a prophylactic dose.

Crossing the city was an extremely social activity.  As there were so many of us, we would meet a friend of at least one member of the party on each street corner.  One of these was a young woman student of mine from Sagar, Miss Aruna, who was shyly delighted to see me and invited us to lunch the next day in the nearby village where her family kept an Ayurvedic pharmacy.

The last time I had seen my students was six weeks earlier when they were packing to come home after the end of year exams.  Those in their Final year were now anxiously waiting for the telegrams which would tell them if they could put the letters "M.A." after their names.

Telegram delivery seemed a little haphazard.  When we got back to Balu's house there was one waiting for Shibili, who didn't live there, but none for Balu.  Shibili was pleased to learn he had passed with second class honours, but Balu was very worried.  Why was there no telegram for him?  Had his gone to the wrong address?  Was the University saving the "fail" telegrams for last?  He was rather subdued during an otherwise festive supper served up by his old grandmother – who struck me as a great character, making all the boys laugh at jokes which I obviously couldn't understand. In turn, I too managed to keep the party amused.

And so back to Shibili's by taxi and to bed.

Next morning, we had planned to visit the Varkala Canal – part of a major waterway which had been constructed in the 18th and 19th centuries to link the regions of Travancore.  The canal has since fallen into disuse and decay, but though most traffic had already passed to rail and road, there were still some freight boats plying the canal in 1968.  Now, in 2017, there is a major project to restore it as a tourist attraction.

This time we didn't bother with a taxi, but walked over to Balu's house across rather hilly ground and I was exhausted on arrival.  A group of students and friends assembled – all boys of course - and we walked over the hill to where the canal enters the 722 metre Sivagiri Tunnel.  After pausing to appreciate the view, we scrambled down to the canal-side, where we hoped to hitch a ride on a boat.

Sivagiri tunnel entrance from above...

We waited a couple of hours before one came.  It was an old wooden boat made of planks stitched together with twine, carrying a load of sea-shells – which I suppose were to be ground up for fertilizer - and propelled by a single boatman with a pole.  We all climbed on board, and Prasad, one of the boys, helped with the punting.

It was a dark, eerie trip through the tunnel, with water dripping from the ceiling.  Midway there was a deep ventilation shaft and as we looked up we saw hundreds of bats circling against the distant sky.  As we went through, we kept our spirits up by singing and shouting.

I had had a great time with this group and was once again overwhelmed by the welcome.  I asked them when they were coming to England, though felt rather insincere doing so, as I thought at the time that they would never be able to.  I had of course no inkling of the banalization of air transport, the economic development of India or the Indian diaspora which would occur over the subsequent 30 years.

**...and from water-level.**

Next day it was time to move on again.  Shibili took me to Balu's in a taxi, where we were gradually joined by the others.  Balu's telegram had finally arrived and he was happy to learn he too had an M.A. with second class honours.  For my part, I was feeling tired – which I blamed on the anti-histamines I was taking for recurrent hayfever – and rather depressed at having to leave my friends.  So I was very quiet sitting there waiting till it was time to go.  Would my next point of call be as much fun?  We all went together to the bus stand, and waited for some time holding hands or arms around shoulders, but when the bus came I hardly had time to climb aboard before it was off again and I couldn't even say goodbye properly!

## 8. Trivandrum

It was a short 50 km ride to Trivandrum, Kerala's capital.  I was going to stay with Alexander John, another Christian student at Sagar.

On the outskirts of Trivandrum, Alex waved the bus down, climbed up and told me I should please get off.  From there it was only a short walk to his house.

My stay in Trivandrum was short, arriving Saturday lunchtime and leaving on Monday morning.  This wasn't planned – at least by me.  My first impressions were very good – I was welcomed into the family, where Alexander was the eldest of several children.  But it wasn't the free and easy atmosphere of Varkala where I had been swept up into a group of my students.  Alex's father had recently returned from a year or two of working on contract for BP in Kuwait.  I felt there was a distinct competition for the role of head of family - which the father was trying to get back.  There was even competition over whose guest I was – Alex's or his father's!

After lunch, we went to the zoo.

First there was much discussion as to how I should dress. Alex's father thought it would be best if I dressed like 95% of Kerala men in the traditional lungi – which he proposed to lend me.  Almost everyone agreed with this – except Alex, who was one of the 5% minority who insisted on wearing trousers in public.  As I considered myself his guest, and he would be accompanying me, I followed this advice, though reluctantly: after all I had become accustomed to going out in Indian dress in the north.  This was more comfortable in hot weather and had not caused me any problems.

Somebody in the family also remarked on the fact that I didn't shave my armpits.

"Why do you not shave under your arms, sir? It is more hygienic and more comfortable in hot weather!"

I replied that it had never occurred to me – and wasn't something men did in my country.  In fact, I hadn't noticed until then that all the men in Kerala had clean-shaven armpits.  When in Rome… So I tried it.  I don't know if it was more hygienic, but it certainly wasn't more comfortable – I had red, itching, prickly armpits for several days – and have never repeated the experience.

The food was very tasty, though the family were worried it might not be to my taste.  After supper, I entertained the children by singing and playing on my recorder, and Alex's father showed us his slides of Kuwait.

On Sunday we were up at seven in order to go to Church.  This was just across the road.  The denomination was Syrian Catholic and the church was modern, with paintings of evangelists and seraphim in shades of brown.  Shoes were left outside as in a temple or mosque and though there were a few seats for the old and infirm, the congregation sat mainly on the floor.

It was Whit Sunday – Festival of the Holy Spirit and I found the service interminable.  Because of the language barrier I couldn't follow the liturgy, but was struck by the frequent opening and closing of a curtain in front of the sanctuary – was this the "veil of the temple"?

In the afternoon we went out for a drive with some of Alex's friends to see the sights.  We visited a large temple, but I was denied access.  In principle one had to be a practising Hindu, but in practise to be bare-chested and wearing a lungi. In the evening I had plenty of time to myself to catch up on my diary for the previous few days.  I was even lent a typewriter on which I started a long letter home which would be continued over the next few days.

A letter from my parents had been waiting for me at Mathew's house in Ernakulum. It contained press cuttings about the furore surrounding the Labour Government's Race Relations Bill, designed to make it illegal to refuse housing, employment, or public services on the grounds of colour, race, ethnic or national origins. As the bill was being debated, A thousand dockers had marched on Parliament in support of racist right-wing M.P. Enoch Powell, sacked from the Tory Shadow Cabinet after his infamous "Rivers of Blood" speech in Birmingham. I wrote back:

*"I am glad to see you are espousing the anti-Powell cause. I can just imagine you both button-holing passengers on the buses.... 'What do you think of these dockers? I think Powell should be made to live with them etc.' I hope you don't get into any fights. Do I detect a certain liberalising of Mum's attitude since I came out here?*

*Really all this Powell business does make me feel very bad Everyone is so kind and welcoming here and I know they would not be treated so well if they came to England."*

I had been planning to visit Ceylon and went to the Tourist Office in Trivandrum on Monday morning to find out the procedure. The employee there explained that as I was not on a short term tourist visa, but had been working in India, I wasn't allowed to leave the country without first obtaining a certificate from the income tax authorities.

"It's very simple. You must ask your employer for a statement of all your income and your tax status, then you take this with your passport to the Tax office in town centre and they will give you necessary certificate."

Not so simple as that: my employer was four days' journey to the North and not renowned for bureaucratic rapidity. Oh yes – and my passport was nestling in the English department safe, also four days' to the North. I decided to change my plans and head down to Cape Comorin instead.

The tension in my host family was becoming rather oppressive and I couldn't make the situation out. Alexander kept encouraging me to move on as soon as possible, whereas his father was eager for me to stay a few more days. I seemed to be in the middle of some family drama, so decided to leave them to it.  I thanked them profusely for their hospitality and struck out again on my own.

I had enjoyed my time in Kerala.  It struck me as generally richer, cleaner and more egalitarian than much of India.  Life was simple, but I saw none of the squalor and grinding poverty I was used to in the North – and would see again in the State of Madras. The only beggars I saw were immigrants from the North and as far as I can remember, the middle-class families I stayed with didn't have servants, though they were sending their children to Universities far away.  Nature was kind, with lush vegetation everywhere and the climate neither oppressively hot nor cold.

# 9. Land's end -Kanyakumari

Beyond the city of Nagercoil in Madras State[8], Kanyakumari - Cape Comorin in English – Is the southern tip of India.

*Kumari* means "maiden" and this rocky promontory is named for and sacred to the maiden goddess Kanniya – known in other manifestations as Durga or Kali.  On one of the two small islands off the point, local legend has it that the goddess lived an austere life in ancient times.  On pilgrimage to her temple here, Swami Vivekanand, the 19th century monk who was a leading figure in both the Hindu Revival and the Nationalist Movement and who introduced Hinduism to the Western world, is said to have received enlightenment.

There has been much building here in the last 50 years. Recent photographs show a multi-coloured built-up area where temples and hotels jostle for a view of the islands in the bay, one dominated by the monumental Vivekenand Memorial Centre, the other by a 40-metre-high statue of Tamil poet and philosopher Tiruvalluvar.

What I remember is a fishing village on a wild windswept headland.  There were a number of memorials and small temples dotted over it and along the beach – the two largest being an old temple with a high outside wall painted in huge vertical red and white stripes and what I considered "a rather ghastly Gandhi memorial".  The Cape's role as a place of pilgrimage entitled it to a small railway station on an extension of the line from Madras to Nagercoil.  There was also an imposing Catholic Church, Our Lady of Ransom, built in 1900 on the site of a much older church.  I was told that most of the fishermen are Catholics and have been since the visit of St Francis Xavier in 1542.  200 metres out to sea, on the rock which bears his name, work had recently started on the Memorial to Vivekananda.

---

[8] Now Tamilnadu.

As for accommodation, there were two possibilities: one was a dharmsala or pilgrim "inn" run by the local Madras State Government. This was free of charge but very basic. The alternative, which my friends in Trivandrum had recommended, was the recently opened Kerala House – a guesthouse run by the Kerala State Government charging five rupees a night. I chose the latter, which proved to be one of the most imposing buildings in town and I was amazed to be shown into an enormous, lofty, well-appointed room complete with bathroom, toilet and dressing room. My five-rupee suite had about the same living space as my entire council-house home in England.

After checking in and taking a quick shower, I went out for a walk along the beach. I was hoping to see the sun set into the Arabian sea, but at this time of year, near its northern limit, it sets into the land. The weather was fine, with a brisk breeze which bent the palm trees and kept the temperature down. Along the way, I got into conversation with an Indian seminary student – who to my surprise defended the American military presence in Vietnam.

As we went on, the sand kept changing colour – red, yellow, black, and the beach was dotted with large boulders.

"You see these big stones?" my companion asked.

"Yes."

"They are from Himalaya."

He paused for effect and I looked surprised and no doubt incredulous, but said nothing, waiting for an explanation.

"That is what local Hindu people say.  You have read Hindu epic *Ramayana*?"

"No, but I've heard of it."

So he went on to relate an incident from the war between Rama, avatar of the god Vishnu and Ravana the demon king in Lanka – modern Sri Lanka, or as it was called in colonial times Ceylon.  Rama's younger brother Laxman had been fatally wounded.  All that could save him was the magic herb sanjeevani which grew only on one mountain in the Himalayas, far to the North. Rama's lieutenant, the monkey god Hanuman, strong, fearless, loyal, decisive but not known for his intellectual prowess, was sent to fetch it. He flew north faster than the wind, found the mountain but couldn't find the plant, so uprooted the whole mountain and flew back carrying it in one hand, occasional bits dropping off along the way – including the spot where we were standing.

Back at the Guesthouse, I had an excellent dinner with a couple of boys from Bombay who were on a tour of the South, then turned in as I planned to be up for the sunrise.

After a night disturbed by hay fever and howling wind, I rose at 5.30 when there was just a little light and walked down in my pajamas, past a few locals defecating on the beach, to the temple at the point. The wind was now so strong I feared my pajama buttons would be ripped off.

On the temple's terrace wall, I sat to watch the sunrise in company with a small band of pilgrims and tourists. To my left was India, ahead the fishing harbour and the Bay of Bengal, to my right the Indian Ocean stretching away toward the Antarctic, at my back the temple and the Arabian Sea. Bats were whizzing about in the pre-dawn gloom, dashing towards the sea wall and away again.

As I waited, Kipling's lines from *Mandalay* kept running romantically through my head:

"And the dawn comes up like thunder out of China across the Bay!"

But it couldn't and didn't. Couldn't because the island of Ceylon and a lot of water were in the way and didn't because there was low cloud on the horizon, so we didn't even see the sun rise from the sea. Just before dawn, however, there was a sudden brightening and everything became suffused with pink – a lovely effect over the small harbour with the boats. Then the sun slowly began to peep through the barring clouds and after ten minutes showed through bright orange and very large. It was a sight worth coming for.

Beside me was a North Indian family. Father and son, both wearing dhotis in the intricate northern style, were busy filming and taking photos of the sunrise – a much more technical undertaking than it would be today.  The father operated the still and film cameras and the son read off from a hand-held light meter as the light changed.  They were so busy recording the scene that I don't think they actually saw it.

The fishermen had prepared their craft and set out as soon as there was enough light.  I wrote home that evening:

*The spot is very exposed and must be most inhospitable in foul weather.  As it is, the wind is strong and full of sand. Nevertheless, the fishermen make a living, and we saw them setting out across the wind in their ridiculous small boats. These are made of four palm trunks lashed together, and though they cannot sink, are most unstable.  Four men stand on a boat, balancing it and punting it out through the shallows.  They then hoist a triangular sail and shoot the gap between the island and the mainland (which is quite rocky).  We saw about a hundred such boats set out in half an hour between us and the rapidly brightening sky.  The mast is elastic and held by a rope at the top so it can be quickly adjusted.*

As I left the beach, four dogs emerged from the skirts of a blind beggar woman and came for me with teeth bared like the hell hounds in *Paradise Lost*.  I stood my ground and luckily this was enough to cow them.

Later that morning, I walked out with my camera to take pictures of the boats and the village.  The boats made a lasting impression on me - solid and frail at the same time.  Wherever I looked at sea I saw them – often as small black dots in the distance.

**Kanyakumari fishing boats at sea...**

**...and on dry land**

I met a group of 5 students from Trivandrum – nice friendly boys - and we spent most of the day together.  After climbing up to the lighthouse to get a general view of the area, we took a free ride out to the Vivekenand Rock with some workmen.  We were in a rather bigger, more secure boat than those mentioned above: it had a hull and a keel, so we sat in it rather than kneeling on it, but it had the same kind of triangular sail and the boatmen had quite a struggle against the rough water, with desperate rowing to avoid being cast up on the rocks as we came close to land.

On the island we saw the men working on the foundations and also a huge footprint- said, depending who you asked, to be one foot of a now lost statue of the goddess Kali, or the footprint of the goddess herself.

**Masons working on Vivekenand Memorial**

Back on land we were proudly shown round the temporary dressing workshop where the craftsmen were carving and polishing the stones in intricate patterns prior to assembly on the island.

**Masons' workshop**

We went on to the Gandhi Memorial, built over the spot where some of his ashes were laid before immersion. There is a hole in the roof designed so that a ray of light falls on the memorial stone on Gandhiji's birthday. I described it in my diary as "a weird structure, something between an iced cake and a rocket launching pad in yellow and blue, much more tasteful inside."

Lastly the boys invited me to the dharmsala or "inn" where they had stayed the night. It was state-owned, absolutely free, but all you got was shelter and a space on the floor to spread your bedding. There were no fittings or restaurant facilities and even cleaning was apparently the responsibility of the visitors or pilgrims, so it was rather grim and filthy. I didn't regret having opted for two nights of splendid isolation in Kerala House!

After leaving them, I continued walking around, now plagued by children begging and selling peanuts & shell necklaces.

**Kanyakumari harbour**

**Kanyakumari village from the sea with Our Lady of Ransom Church and fishing boats**

On Wednesday morning I woke at 5.30, bathed, collected my packed breakfast, paid my bill – Rs 22.36 for two days' excellent full board and walked ten minutes to the station, where I took the 7.00 am Express to Madurai.

# Heading North - Volunteer India

## 10. Boys' Town and well-boring

The Cape was a turning point in more ways than one.  Having reached the southernmost tip of the sub-continent, I was now heading North, back "home" to Sagar.  I had come down along the Western Malabar Coast and would go back more to the East, parallel to the Coromandel Coast.

My accommodation and social context would be different too.  I had spent a cosmopolitan week in the metropolis of Bombay, staying in a luxurious expatriate flat and moving in overlapping upper level business, administrative and artistic circles peopled equally by Europeans and Indians.  This had been followed by three weeks as guest in the homes of ordinary middle-class Indians who were keen to show me the daily life and culture of their country. I often had the impression that in doing so they were discovering things themselves.

I was now entering a microcosm which was still run on a day to day level by Europeans. I would be staying mainly with European Aid workers and missionaries, getting a feel of the wider international Development movement of which in theory I was a part.

From Kanyakumari to Madurai, ancient capital of Tamil culture, is about 250 km.  My train was slow, taking a winding route and stopping frequently, so the journey took about nine hours.  My coach was modern and comfortable, with smoked glass and a supply of drinking water but it was still a very hot journey through the rural areas and small towns of what was still called Madras State.  I was impressed by the number and varied shapes of the temples we passed – some entirely open air, around a central lingam, the stylized cylindrical stone phallus which represents the god Shiva.

We arrived at Madurai Main Station at about 4 p.m.. As usual, I had to fight off a crowd of rickshaw pullers and little boys eager to carry my bags:

"You go Travellers' Bungalow? – this way – I take box."

This time, however, I had another plan. My little address book supplied by VSO in Bombay listed two volunteers in Madurai, at "Boys' Town, Madurai 1" – an entry which sounded both intriguing and reasonably central. I also had a telephone number.

First I wandered around for ten minutes looking for a telephone - one little boy still trailing me, though I had told him to go away.

I ended up in the main Post Office, but I couldn't get through, even though the helpful clerks called their colleagues at the nearest Post Office to Boys' Town. They were determined to help me and had decided they knew how:

"You just take a 21 bus and ask to be put down at Nagalumai."

I tried, knowing in my heart that it was hopeless, to use subtler questioning.

"Yes, thank you, but I don't even know if my friends are there. How easy is it to get to this place?"

"Just take the 21 bus."

"Do you know if the institution is open at the moment? I know we're in the school holidays."

"This boy will show you the bus. Give him your bags."

At this point, I gave up, thanked them and followed my young porter to the bus stand, where he put me into a bus and I gave him four annas. This didn't please him and he made a scene, protesting in hurt tones that he had been guiding me for over an hour and appealing in Tamil to the other passengers. I stood my ground and they took my side, telling him in no uncertain terms to be satisfied and to be off.

I quickly learned that I had the wrong address – Boys' Town was in Madurai 16, on the outskirts, not Madurai 1 - and that in any case, I was on the wrong bus.

We were taken right out into the country and I was told to get down by an alighting passenger who then pointed to a track and said:

"Boys' Town".

"How far?" I asked.

"Four miles[9]."

And he left me by the roadside with my suitcase, my haversack and my umbrella.

I tried to strike up conversation with some passers-by, but they had no English and I no Tamil. I was beginning to get a bit desperate and had more or less decided to wait for the next bus back into town – but when might that be? A small car was approaching, with men in Western dress – potential interpreters! I flagged it down. And the occupants were very helpful.

"But you are on wrong road. Please get in!"

They gave me a lift to a fork in the road a few kilometres on.

"Here you can catch bus to Boys' Town."

"How far is it from the road on this side? – is it beside the road? Do you know when the next bus is?"

But they obviously thought I was fishing for a lift all the way and cut the conversation short.

"You take the bus here and ask for Boys Town."

And they left me. This was a village of sorts and a couple of boys a little younger than me invited me into the tea-stand and bought me coffee. We chatted for a bit, they understood my problem and they arranged with a truck driver that I could ride in the back with the workmen he was taking home and that one of the men should carry my bags and show

_______________________

[9] i.e. 6.5 km. India still used imperial measures.

me the way.  I climbed up and we drove on to another village. The workman supposed to be my porter found a young boy – perhaps 12 years old – to whom he delegated the task, fixing the remuneration in advance.   I felt a little guilty handing my bags to someone so much smaller than me, but the boy seemed delighted to be earning a little money.

The village was full of life.  As we walked up the main street, we met a great crowd escorting a procession.  It must have been a fertility ritual, for the central interest was a double line of women walking along with pots on their heads from which sprouted some kind of cereal.

We walked on down the road for half a mile or so until we came to a track with a board saying "Boys Town".  On the way we were stopped by a peasant woman and a little boy.  The mother pointed at her son and made it obvious by sign language that she wanted me to take him with me.  She wanted to abandon him to the orphanage.  Also using apologetic sign language, I refused.

After another mile of track, during which we saw neither pedestrian nor vehicle, my boy seemed to be wilting a little.  He obviously had diarrhoea, as he kept stopping to defecate among the shrubbery. Eventually, he swallowed his professional pride and let me carry one of my own bags.

We rounded a bend in the track and saw some new buildings. Could this be it?  The light was beginning to fail and they looked suspiciously dark and deserted, but we came nearer and found a sign in English:

"Boys' Town farm – Keep Left"

Avoiding the non-existent traffic, we followed the direction.

On the veranda of the nearest building, I found an athletic young American lying suntanned and naked on a bed. Seeing us, he stood up to greet me, rapidly wrapping a towel around himself.

"Hi there.  I'm Brother Tom. Sorry about the informal dress, but I've got a bit of fever."

He was the most unmonkish brother I have ever met.

"I'm looking for a couple of British volunteers …"

"Oh, yes, I know them.  You see those buildings across the field?  You should find them there."

"I was wondering if I could stay the night," I ventured.

"You'll have to," he replied.  "Be dark in ten minutes."

So I crossed a couple of fields to Boys' Town proper, where I would stay for a couple of days.  I paid my guide and he slipped away into the night.

I introduced myself and was immediately welcomed.  It was the end of the day, and the staff were gathering in the common room.  The radio was on and the atmosphere was heavy.  News was coming in of the shooting of presidential candidate Bobby Kennedy in Los Angeles.

The institution was run by a handful of Christian Brothers with the help of four volunteers: two VSO, one independent British, one Danish.  They took in young orphaned or destitute boys, fed them, taught them, trained them in a craft.  The buildings were simple, but brick-built and solid. There were well-equipped metalwork and woodwork workshops where they made furniture for sale and nice residential quarters for both children and staff.  They apparently received significant funding from a German charity.  Their farm specialised in pigs and they had recently opened a bacon factory.

There was another VSO volunteer staying there at the time.  This was Dave Oakes[10], a big strong motherable sort of boy my age from Warrington, 15 km down the road from my home in Rainhill.  He was an engineer working on a practical well-boring project in the region.  He was also a keen

---

[10] Whilst correcting the proofs of this volume, I have been contacted by Dave after losing contact for 50 years!  He has sent me a copy of the report he wrote on returning to the UK.

mountaineer and a 200m fall into a deep snowdrift in the Cairngorms had left him uninjured apart from an unfortunate stammer on the letter "B".

"What do you do?"

"B-b-b-boring."

He had managed to keep news of his accident from his mother and I have kept his secret for nearly 50 years, but I suppose there is no longer any need.

We immediately hit it off together and he invited me to visit his project the next day.

I rose at six, washed my clothes in the bathroom and we set off together on Dave's battered Honda motorbike to the ashram where he was working on a well.

VSO supplied bikes where this was considered essential for a volunteer's project, but were institutionally paranoid about safety, insisting that volunteers always wear helmets.  This was totally reasonable but unenforceable and there were occasional accidents and even deaths.  I remember feeling very awkward a few years later when as a VSO desk officer I had to speak to the parents of a volunteer who had died this way in Thailand.

"Have you got a second helmet?" I asked Dave.

"Don't even wear one myself," he replied. "You can't wear a helmet in this heat!"

As anyone who has been to India knows, the horn is considered an essential driving aid, constantly announcing one's approach to other road users – including cattle. He didn't have one of those that worked either.

"Hop on!" said Dave.

"Umm, I've never been on a motorbike before.  What do I actually do?"

"Er, nothing really.  Just sit and lean the same way I do. Hold onto me if it makes you feel better!"

So we bumped and swayed down eight kilometres of potholed dirt tracks to an ashram recently taken over by Hindu monks, followers of the same 19th century Swami Vivekenand whose memorial I had seen being built at the Cape. They had opened a small school and planned to be self-sufficient in foodstuffs, so were bringing the surrounding fields under irrigation. The existing wells were insufficient, so they had approached Dave's outfit, which as a non-profit organisation, was the cheapest operator in the business.

Perhaps it is worth trying at this juncture to make some sense of the complex and confusing rural development scene in 60's India.

The international context was that of post-colonial Third World Development and Aid movements. European powers were trying to redefine their relationship to their former "possessions". Newly independent countries were trying to find their own way. Their leaders were variously seeking to improve the lives of their fellow citizens or trying to find ways of lining their own pockets. International bodies such as the WHO, World Bank and UNICEF were becoming increasingly involved. Non-colonial powers and international business were jostling for influence and competing to offer technical, financial and military aid. Sometimes the results were grotesque and the most extreme example is the USA "winning the hearts and minds" of Vietnam's villagers by spraying them with napalm.

Two decades after Independence, India was in a three-year lull between Five Year Plans. The third FYP – generally considered unsuccessful - had ended in 1966 and the fourth had yet to be promulgated. The vast majority of the country's people lived in rural areas, often in great poverty and Indira Gandhi's Congress Government was keen to support rural development and what was called the "Green Revolution". At national and local levels there was a growing interest in self-sufficiency and such movements as *Gramdan*, which encouraged landowners to donate parcels of land to the poor.

Though there was national government support in principle, there was an administrative vacuum on the ground. This vacuum was filled by an interlocking mixture of heterogeneous home-grown and foreign organisations, both secular and religious, of widely differing sizes, many of very recent foundation.

So where did Dave and I fit into all this, as we bounced along the dirt-track that June morning in '68?

We had both been recruited and sent out to India by Voluntary Service Overseas in London, a charity founded in 1958 to provide a useful replacement for National (military) Service. VSO had matched us to projects recommended by their "Overseas Arm" the British Council, a quasi-governmental body whose main objective was to promote British culture overseas.

My case was relatively simple: my head of project, a University Professor of English, had long been in contact with the British Council, who had provided his scholarship to study at a British University. He simply asked for a recently qualified English graduate and I was taken on a temporary contract and paid by the Indian University Grants Commission at the same rate as an Indian junior lecturer.

Dave's was more complex. Having recently completed an apprenticeship with the Warrington engineering firm Electro-Hydraulics Ltd., he had persuaded his employers to release and sponsor him on VSO. This meant they kept a job open for him and continued to pay his National Insurance contributions while he was in India.[11]   Via the British Council representative in

---

[11] The report Dave wrote for his employers on returning to the UK ends, "During my stay, I drilled about 150 wells and in only two did I find no water… I wish to thank the Board of Directors for giving me the opportunity to help directly and in a small way some of the millions of underprivileged and often starving Indians. The Well Boring Project, operated by Voluntary Service Overseas Volunteers in conjunction with various religious missions, is a really worthwhile cause.  In giving help to these people less fortunate than ourselves, one obtains in return a greater confidence in oneself and a broader outlook towards one's own job and life in general."

Hyderabad, and an arcane expat mafia, he was posted with half a dozen others to work for Action for Food Production or AFPRO, an NGO "established in 1966 with Christian inspiration, as a secular Indian technical service organization"[12]. After six months boring wells for rich farmers around Hyderabad, he was reposted to Madurai. Here, AFPRO's Water Well Boring project was managed by an American missionary, Charles Heinemann, who had been in India for 20 years. AFPRO was Dave's local employer, paying him at the local rate and Charles was his direct boss. Charles ran two drilling teams, each headed on a two-year contract by a British volunteer, whose job was to train local workers who it was hoped would become autonomous. Dave's apprentices were three youngsters from Boys' Town – an orphanage run with volunteer help by American Christian Brothers with German charitable funding…

AFPRO's well-boring project was partly financed by the British NGO Oxfam (founded as Oxford Committee for Famine Relief in 1942), which provided capital investment: tractors and drilling equipment. Oxfam had been active in India since 1965 and in 1968 had just appointed its first Field Director there to create the Oxfam Gramdan Action Programme, which "would be the first joint rural development programme in Oxfam history and the first step to a new 'operational' Oxfam"[13].

The aim of the project was to develop agriculture in the area by boring new irrigation wells, or by improving existing ones. The current customer was an ashram and school, run by the Vivekenanda Trust, a Hindu charitable institution with both religious and political agendas.

Is all that clear? Shall I start again?

---

[12] Afpro.org website.
[13] Wikipedia « Oxfam »

We arrived at the Ashram and were greeted by a swami with shaven head and saffron robes, who I learned was supervising the proceedings.

Dave's three boys were already there. I presume they had spent the night at the ashram, guarding the 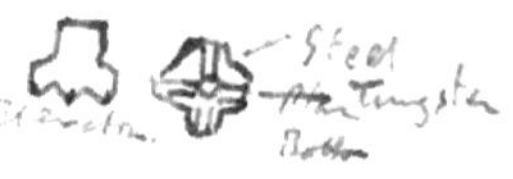 equipment against pilfering. They were very young, slim but fit. Two struck me as about 14 or 15 and the eldest, who was being trained as foreman, maybe 16, but they were probably a bit older. I was only 22 myself and I think Dave was 23. He had been doing this job for nearly two years and would return home to Warrington in a couple of months.

They were working at the bottom of an old water tank about seven metres deep. They had hit good water at about three and a half metres the previous day and were now going to try a second hole. They pumped out the new water, but it was very muddy in the tank, which hadn't been cleaned for ten years and was full of black sludge. We would all get filthy before the day was out.

I was fascinated by the ingenious Heath Robinson style drilling method. First, a two-foot long steel pipe[14] was driven into the ground as a guide for the drill bit. Then the tungsten steel bit was driven into the ground on the end of hollow steel rods by an adapted hand-held road drill suspended on a rope from a pulley. The whole system was operated by compressed air from a compressor on the tractor at ground level above.

It was a two-boy job: one held the drill with both hands, the other took part of its weight on the rope. As the drill operator had a very limited range – from head to thigh level - it was

---

[14] For simplicity, I leave these measures in the old Imperial Units which have since been abandoned almost everywhere except the USA. For those to whom they are strange, 1 foot (ft.) = 30.5 cm. As a very rough guide, three feet are about one metre.

necessary to repeat a tedious sequence of operations with rods of different lengths, screwed together:

1. drill with 2 ½ foot rod,
2. pull back;
3. unscrew and replace 2 ½ with 5 ft. rod
4. drill another 2 ½ feet,
5. pull back;
6. Repeat 2 - 4  with 7 ½ and 10 ft rods.
7. 10 ft rod stays in hole, add 2 ½ ft. rod
8. Repeat 1 – 7 until you hit water…

This was slow, but it worked.  Dave told me it drilled a 5 cm. hole and was effective down to about 20 metres – not the 40 metres claimed by the inventors.

He reckoned it wasn't really suited to local conditions, but it was what Oxfam had given them. In theory it was an inexpensive low-tech system adapting easily available equipment, but they had great difficulty getting spare parts. They were also given no money for maintenance or running costs, so had to charge for their services which meant that the really poor farmers didn't benefit.

**In the tank. Upper level: Swami, Dave, boy foreman.
Lower level: junior boys.**

Dave's team of three lads from Boys' Town was supposed to carry on alone when he left in August, but he was pessimistic about this:

"They won't be ready.  They work really hard, but they lack initiative.  They don't realise something is going wrong until it's too late!"

It says something about the quality of the Boys' Town teaching, however, that these rural orphans could follow Dave's training.  This must have been in English, as at the time VSO didn't believe in teaching local languages to their volunteers!

During the morning, Dave's boss Charles, a thin ascetic looking man, dropped in by motorbike, wearing a towel wrapped round his head as a turban.

He was very upset about Bobby Kennedy.

"You've heard he died in the hospital?  What's the country coming to?"

Then we discussed Oxfam, with whom he was finding it difficult working:

"The trouble is that they don't trust the knowledge and experience of the people working in the field."

After Charles left, Dave told me how fond he was of him:

"He's a really great man to work for.  He lets you get on with it, but he's always there if you need him.  And he'll get down in the hole with you himself and get his hands dirty."

The team worked hard till about 4.30 when the tractor engine driving the compressor sputtered to a stop.

"B-b-b-bugger! Tank's empty.  It was full yesterday morning. Someone must have siphoned some off!"

**Boys drilling.**

Dave got a jerry-can of diesel from the ashram and tried to bleed the air from the engine, but without success. It had started to rain, so we called it a day.

We headed back to Boys' Town through a downpour, now splashing and slithering between the flooded potholes. My first two pillion rides had been quite an experience! Fortunately, Dave was by now an expert at riding in these conditions and I proved to have natural balance and did nothing to hinder his control of the machine.

The rain had washed most of the mud off but we still had a shower. The downpour was short-lived and after supper, the air now relatively cool, we climbed back on his bike and went into Madurai to catch the 10.15 showing of *One Million Years B.C.* This was the amazing 1966 Hammer Films production starring Raquel Welch as the ultimate volunteer: an under-dressed and firm-breasted cavewoman leading her troglodyte people to survive assaults by giant pterodactyls and cataclysmic earthquakes. Tamil subtitles were unnecessary, as there was no language except a few words of the "Ugh…ugh! Aargh!" variety.

One film-goer confessed to me at the interval: "Is very interesting film, but I am having difficulty understanding dialogue. It is because the actors are speaking with American accent."

We got back to Boys' Town about 1.30 and I found there was a strange white boy sleeping in "my" bed, so I slept out on the verandah.

In the morning, I discovered this was Geoff Rich, the schoolboy son of a US AID officer attached to the American Embassy in Delhi. Geoff had come down to help out at Boys' Town during his holidays and had somehow managed to arrive in the dark while Dave and I were at the cinema.  He must have been about 16.  It strikes me as I write this that in the society I live in now, the only people of such an age to behave with this level of autonomy are members of the so-called deprived or criminal classes!

Geoff had been detailed to help Ian on the farm and I volunteered to help there too.  Ian himself was a sort of "unofficial VSO" who had come out alone from England to a nearby project, soon got to hate his boss and had moved to Boys' Town, where he had been helping Brother Tom on the farm for the last five weeks in return for board and lodging.  Brother Tom's "bit of fever" had turned out to be hepatitis and he had been taken to hospital the day before, leaving Ian in charge.

There was no shortage of manpower at Boys' Town. By the time we got over to the farm, all the day-to-day tasks were being done by boys, so Ian asked us to mark out a provisional site for a pig-muck dump.  One pig apparently produced about 250 kilos of shit a week and they had a hundred pigs.

This job didn't take us long and I quickly realised that there was nothing really for me to do here.  Luckily, I was in the common room at lunchtime when a certain Dora Scarlett called in.  She was a vigorous woman in her early sixties who was running a nearby village development centre and clinic called Seva Nilayam or "Place of Service".

"Do you need any help?" I asked her. "I'm free for a few days, if you can use me."

"Oh yes, please.  Come whenever you can.  I'll find things for you to do!"

Dave came back from the Ashram at about three, saying he had to go to town to meet a man from the BBC who wanted to make a film about him.

"Why don't you come with me?  You can stay with Charles for a couple of nights.  There's nothing for you to do here."

So I packed quickly and we left.

Charles was happy to see me again – and to put me up, even lend me money.  I found him a strange man.  His house was full of paper and plastic spheres, which he made himself and which dangled around at head level.  His bookshelves were full of books on religion and philosophy and his back yard full of well-boring equipment.

It turned out that Dave's "BBC man" was an independent film producer making a publicity documentary about British volunteers for showing in universities, factories etc. as a recruitment aid.  I don't know who was paying for this.  Charles was planning to drive him out to Seva Nilayam the next day to meet Dora and he offered me a lift.

## 11. Seva Nilayam

Charles drove and I chatted with the film director, an easy-going middle aged man whose name I haven't noted.   A week before, he had been in Iran, failing for the second time to meet a volunteer who this time was cut off by floods and in January had been cut off by snowdrifts. Before that, he had been in Botswana, where he had interviewed my old school friend Adam Green, who was a volunteer there.

"Small world!" I said.

"Yes, isn't it!"

"What's your plan here?"

"We are going to do a four-minute segment with your friend Dave and his team drilling a well in the courtyard of the children's home."

"Dora has a volunteer nurse working there as well," said Charles.

"Really?  That's good!  Maybe I can work her in for good measure."

The setting was beautiful - a flat, dusty plain, surrounded on all sides by hills and mountains – what I imagined Australia might look like.  We drove through the heat for a couple of hours on progressively worse roads, through smaller and poorer towns and villages.

Suddenly, we came to green fields of stout green dwarf maize.

"We've arrived," said Charles. "This is the demonstration farm.  You'll meet Mr. Reddy who runs it."

Then we turned off the main track at a little stall which sold recycled medicine bottles to patients and a hundred yards more and we were into the courtyard.

The place was full of life. In front of me was the ideal "missionary" picture – a young white nurse was giving treatment on the verandah while a swarm of natives, mainly children, sat and stood around, waiting, watching and sometimes wailing. I would soon learn that the colonial or missionary overtones of this image were far from the spirit of Seva Nilayam.

**Queue at clinic, Seva Nilayam 1968**

Workmen were building a new outbuilding out of wooden poles and coconut fronds. The other buildings were more solid mud and brick affairs – rather like the Irish cottages I had stayed in in my childhood, but with tiled roofs instead of thatch.

Plans were made for the filming –

"Miss Scarlett, I hope you realise that the film is about volunteers – not about your clinic, which is only a setting – some people are terribly disappointed afterwards."

Coffee was drunk, mango eaten and the film-director produced a tape recorder and started to interview Jean, the volunteer nurse. At this point, an urgent call came - by runner, there was no telephone - that a village woman had thrown herself into the fire in an epileptic fit, so Charles's car was pressed into service as an ambulance and Dora and Jean, set off with a big black bag.

**Dora dancing with Mahalingam, Mani at right.**

Dora Scarlett was 63. She had quit Europe, taken her savings and come to South India "Just like that!" nine years earlier. After meeting Seetharam Reddy and his wife and finding they had similar ideas, the three of them set out to find a place where they could put those ideas into practice. In 1962, they started Seva Nilayam.

Dora had been disillusioned by both organized religion and organized politics. From a modest Catholic background in Liverpool, she had turned to Communism and as a Party member was sent as an English language broadcaster to Radio Budapest. She quit Hungary and the Communist Party during the Soviet suppression of the 1956 Uprising.

All she brought from Communism was the basic Marxist dogma "From each according to his abilities, to each according to his needs", which I think I heard for the first time from her mouth.  She was a strong believer in self -sufficiency, in keeping things small and local, in using the best of traditional methods and in not imposing foreign ideas.  She had known Mahatma Gandhi in 1930's London and agreed with many of his principles.

She dressed as a local woman, had learned to speak the local version of Tamil and came across as a strong personality, but simple and loving in a no-nonsense sort of way – what is sometimes known as "tough love".

The centre she founded with the Reddys still exists[15].  It has much developed from the small operation I saw, changing to respond to changing local needs – responding for instance to the problems of HIV and AIDS.  I believe Dora was still giving advice from her wheelchair at the age of 95, a few weeks before she died in 2001!


I stayed at Seva Nilayam for nearly a week.

When the clinic was busy, patients were received by Jean, the medical assistant Nagaraj and sometimes Dora herself while I helped in the background, counting out pills, cutting up rolls of gauze and folding it to make compresses etc.

We had been given lots of small sample bottles of pills.  These I emptied into larger vessels, thus recovering useful bottles for dispensing – and a wad of cotton wool from each bottle which could be used for cleaning wounds.  Our level of asepsis was not that of 21$^{st}$ century hospitals, but it didn't need to be.  Superbugs were not yet a problem, ordinary dirt was.

I saw results of great neglect – children covered in sores, wounds gone septic and so on.  Practically everyone had worms.  Whatever the presenting symptoms, there was a standard protocol of questions:

---

[15] For information: http://www.villageservicetrust.org.uk/  or @villageservicetrust on Facebook or Messenger.  This UK charity has supported Seva Nilayam financially for 30 years.

"Do you have diarrhoea?  Any urine trouble?" and for the women, "How many children have you got?"

Problems beyond our limited resources were sent to the hospital in Madurai.  As Seva Nilayam had no vehicles at that time, this usually meant telling the patient to take the bus and giving him or her a letter of referral.  In a real emergency, the patient would be accompanied by whoever was available – usually Nagaraj.

Occasionally I got more directly involved.  For instance, one man came in complaining of an enlarged scrotum.  June – in a delicate position as a woman - was for sending him off to hospital without examining him, but Nagaraj and I thought maybe we should have a look.  What we saw struck us both as fairly normal – I'd have been proud of it!

Apart from helping in the clinic, and occasionally in the kitchen, much of my time was spent clearing the backlog of more intellectual jobs which Dora considered important but not urgent.  I worked for instance on a photo album and also spent considerable time sorting through crates full of USAID medical supplies sent from America to decide if anything was worth keeping. I threw away large quantities of tranquillizers, sleeping pills and Vicks aerosols ("spray around the bedroom to relieve that stuffed-up feeling"), together with bottles of pills with American brand names and the only direction "use as directed by the physician".  What would have been useful – but weren't sent – were vitamins, antibiotics, TB medicines, wormicides … and soap!

Patients coming to the clinic were given soap to wash themselves, but all the clinic could afford was the crude laundry soap used by *dhobis*.  This came in large blocks which we cut up into small pieces.  This hardly produced any lather at all.  I wrote home suggesting my parents contact their local Oxfam branch to persuade soap firms in Liverpool or Widnes to donate more suitable soap.  Something must have come of this, because I have a letter to my mother in Dora's firm elegant hand dated December 1968 saying:

*"... Even if I have not received the parcels, not to worry...*

*Everything takes longer since shipping had to go round the Cape. When I first came here they took 2 to 3 months, now 3 to 5 months. Still, I have no reason to think any parcels are missing. I believe they pile up in some warehouse awaiting Customs examination, and then a lot are released together.*

*As soon as I receive them, I shall write and thank all the people you mention."*

I also played with the children and we became very fond of each other. I picked up a Tamil vocabulary of about ten words – hello, goodbye, yes, no, good, bad... – which I have since forgotten. This was however enough with sign language to get along and even to tell off one little TB patient who I caught spitting into the drinking water tank!

There were about fifteen children staying in the centre, most of whom had been brought in for treatment and stayed till it was complete. Some however were suffering basically from neglect, and having brought them in, their parents showed no further interest in them.

Dora was very concerned about the children who came into her care. Apart from their physical and medical needs, she provided a warm, loving playful environment. She made great efforts to have her long-term charges educated – something rare in the villages at that time, particularly for girls, who were normally destined just for marriage and motherhood – domestic slavery rather than domestic bliss!

She was keen to have the girls learn a trade which would make them financially independent. Before I left, we arranged that I should sponsor Dhanalakshmi, one of her girls, by paying her Training Institute fees for the year.  Dora wrote to me on 12ᵗʰ December:

*"Many thanks for your Money Order for Rs 40 received yesterday.*

*Dhanalakshmi must have taken her sewing exam a few days ago, on the 8ᵗʰ.  I haven't seen her, so I don't know how she got on.  She will be coming here to spend Christmas from the 19ᵗʰ for about a week.*

*If she passes well, as I have every confidence she will, she may stay on at the Institute and start to learn cutting and tailoring.  Then she can take her higher embroidery and lower cutting and sewing exam next December.  She is very happy, developing into a fine young woman, so we shall make an effort to keep her there.*

*I didn't really think you could manage to come so far for Christmas but thought there was no harm in asking. Maybe you will come here before you leave."*

I had been pleased at Dora's invitation for Christmas in a previous letter, but I too had only about a week's holiday and the return journey alone would have meant at least six days in buses and trains!

A lot of the children were very small for their age.  I remember one charming little boy called Mahalingam (which means Shiva of the Great Penis) who struck me as a very bright three or four-year-old and very healthy – but was in fact seven years old. TB of one kind or another was also common.  One little boy called Mani with TB of the spine was very proud of his tub-like plaster cast – inviting people to drum on it.


One evening, Charles Heinemann's other drilling team turned up in an Oxfam Land Rover – four men and a parrot which caused great excitement amongst the Seva Nilayam cats.  Their leader was Rupert Talbot, whom I had last seen at the one-week VSO training course in Tottenham the previous July.  There he had led a chorus of engineering volunteers at the last night concert, singing, "We are from AFPRO, Good boys are we…".

He told me he was happy in his work, but couldn't stand Indian food.

They had started drilling at the leprosy clinic Dora was setting up a few miles away and I went with them next day to watch. This team looked more professional than Dave's. They wore khaki uniforms and were older – man-sized rather than boy-sized. Despite this, Rupert had the same reservations as Dave about their lack of initiative and ability to work alone after he left.

Their equipment was much heavier and more impressive than Dave's hand-drill affair. It was called a Tiger and was designed for test-bores in the UK. I described it as a "sort of workshop on wheels". Its hydraulic jack-hammer went down the hole directly behind the bit.

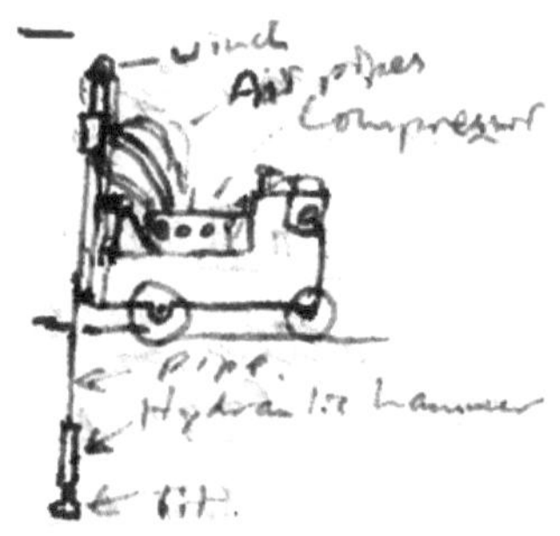


Volunteers had not been impressed with its utility in a Third World rural context and had become great fault-finders. For instance, the compressor was sealed – fine if you were 100 km from the factory, but more difficult if anything went wrong out here. Then, despite weighing two tons, it had no road springs or shock absorbers. This made it exempt from road tax in the UK – where it would be delivered to site on a low-loader - but here it had to be towed behind a Land Rover, which meant very slow driving. Off-road, the land had to be levelled in front of it.

During the morning, Rupert cut his hand and had to be taken back to be patched up by June and in the afternoon, Dora borrowed the farm manager's motorbike and came out, her sari tucked up under her, to watch the drilling.

The local water diviner, a rather pompous man who referred to himself as "Geomantic Research Station Private" on his business card, had indicated the place to drill, but after two days drilling through granite, quartzite and mica and breaking two bits and a piston, there was still no sign of water.

Well past the middle of my summer break, I was still a long way from home.  I had enjoyed my time at Seva Nilayam, feeling I had learnt a lot from Dora – with whom I remained in contact by correspondence – and that I had actually been of some practical help.  I had hoped to be present for the filming, but things were delayed.  The camera crew were still in Bombay, trying to get their film released from Customs. So I told Dora I would be moving on.

"I'm sorry to see you go," she said. "But you can do something useful for us in Madurai."

She explained that they had referred a child who had come to the clinic to the Erskine Hospital with suspected osteomyelitis.  His brother had taken him there with a letter but they had been shunted from room to room seeing no-one and returned dispirited to Dora.

"It's terrible to have to say this," she continued.  "But the medical staff will take more notice of you.  I'll send the boys again tomorrow.  You can meet them off the bus and accompany them to the hospital.  In the meantime, can you try to get in touch with the doctor today and tell him you're coming?"

Feeling a little queasy at the idea of pulling rank in a hospital – the only grounds my middle-class status and white skin – I agreed.

# 12.   Madurai

The bus through the villages took about three hours.  All I had seen of Madurai 10 days earlier was the railway station and the post office, so this time I was determined to do a little sightseeing. I went straight to the Tourist Bungalow and checked in. There I tried to contact the doctor at the hospital but was told he had gone sailing.  They would ask him to ring me back that afternoon.  He didn't and despite several attempts, I never managed to speak to him.

**Gopura (detail)**

Madurai is a temple city and major centre of pilgrimage.  The streets of the old town are laid out in a maze of nesting squares around the enormous Temple to Meenakshi, avatar of Parvati, consort to Shiva.  Built in the 16th and 17th centuries, this is a jewel of Dravidian temple architecture, unusual in being a major temple dedicated to a female deity and the second biggest Hindu temple in India (I would see the biggest a few days later at Tiruchirappalli).  Its most striking feature is the four massive *gopuras* or entrance towers in the middle of the four outer walls facing the cardinal points.  These are adorned by row after row of polychrome statuary and the tallest is 60m high.

Unlike some temples, here I was allowed to enter and wander around quite freely.  I reproduce my enthusiastic naïve non-specialist notes of the time:

**Outer court of temple**

*I returned to Madurai to see the great temple, which is quite fantastic...  Fabulous place, would make an ideal film set!  Massive halls & corridors, images of all sorts, people bathing & sitting round the tank.  Court after court, carved and painted and swarming with happy crowds of worshippers performing puja.  The devotees of Ganesh (the elephant god) are particularly interesting – they cross their hands like this - I think they hold their ears and then they bounce up and down.  Others pour butter into the flames before the idols, or offer garlands of flowers, or break a coconut as offering.  To perform the complete puja, one must come and live in the temple for several days. Many of the others just wander around or sit in groups & talk. There is a big temple tank where they can take a holy dip & there is even a bazaar inside the temple. A real day-out atmosphere!*

*There is a museum of temple art in 1,000 pillar hall. Across the road from the main entrance, the choultry[16] has been turned into a tailors' & haberdashers' bazaar – under the carvings of griffons - sewing machines.*

**Street outside temple with *Gopura***

Next morning, I went to the bus-stand at 7.30 to meet the boys off the bus which called at Seva Nilayam at about 4.30. They weren't on it, so I waited a couple of hours for the next bus. They weren't on that either, so I went to Charles' house to ask him to give a message to Dora and to repay the 20 rupees I owed him.

---

[16] Building offering free lodging to pilgrims.

Charles was getting ready to go to Seva Nilayam.  The crew had arrived from Bombay with the film and shooting would start today.  Charles was taking his own cook John out to feed the troops.

"By the way," he said.  "Dave's trying to get in touch with you.  He's planning to go up to Kody tomorrow."

I spent the rest of the morning in the Gandhi museum nearby.  A number of middle-class Indians I had met at Sagar and in my travels had objected strongly to the picture of India as a starving nation.  Some even went so far as to claim, "There is no poverty in India!"  After Seva Nilayam, I felt more and more that Gandhi was right on many things and that Indians who made such statements were either ignorant of their own country or completely uncaring.

Back at the Tourist Bungalow (Rs 4 a day, meal Rs 1.40) I slept from one to five.  Then Dave phoned.  Forget smartphones – this meant a servant hammering on my door:

"Sir! Sir! Telephone!  Please come to Reception!"

I got up and went.

"I'm going up to Kody for a couple of days with Neils," said Dave. "You met him… the Danish volunteer at Boys' Town.  Do you want to come?"

"Yes, sure.  What time are you leaving tomorrow?"

"Neils wants to go up tonight.  Can you be ready at 6.30?"

"Er… O.K."

"We'll pick you up."

# 13.   Kodaikanal

Night was beginning to fall and the sky was suffused with red as the two motorbikes drew up.  Dave strapped my suitcase behind his big bedroll on the carrier and I climbed on.  It was like riding in an armchair.

Kodaikanal, or Kody for short, is the hill station 120 km from Madurai.  The average June temperature range at Madurai (altitude 101 m) is 26 -38°C.  Kody, at 2,133 m has 12 -19°C.

We went up the narrow mountain road in the dark.  It was enjoyable but quite eventful.  The first excitement was at a filling station where we killed a small but apparently lethal snake which was showing interest in us.  Then Dave narrowly missed going off the road twice at bends.  When I came down by bus in daylight, I wondered how we ever got up.  We were riding through jungle with a large bear population. Three quarters of the way up there was a shrine, where all the lorry drivers – whether Christian or Hindu - stopped to pray and garland the cross.  This marked the spot where a few years earlier a lorry driver had been attacked by a bear when he got down to relieve himself, but prayed to St. Paul (patron saint of sudden meetings on the highway?) and was delivered.

 As we went up, it got colder and colder – and once we had checked in to the well-named Paradise Lodge we kept all our clothes on to sleep.

In the morning, I discovered the amazing view from this mountain lookout.  The ground fell away almost sheer. The cool air was clear and we could see far across ranges of foothills and the vast plain red in the sunlight with all the small hills around Madurai looking quite diminutive.  It was strange to think it was so sweltering down there while we were feeling quite cold.

I must have been feeling a bit homesick and I noted in my diary, "Lovely place, just like England.  Hard to believe it's India."

But it was India.  The hotel dhobi called and I gave him my clothes to wash.  "Clothes ready one o'clock sir!"

We walked up Coaker's Walk, a narrow street lined with bungalows, to Charles' house – aptly named The Lookout.  He and his wife were just leaving for church – it was Sunday – so we said we would call back later.  The town was overflowing with Europeans – in particular schoolgirls.  Modern Kody had in fact been founded in the 19th century by British bureaucrats and American missionaries.  The British had gone, but the Americans were still there.  It was the headquarters of Charles's mission and there was also an American boarding school.

**Dave looking out from Charles' back garden**

Kody has a man-made lake and we went rowing, just as one might in Regent's Park in London.  Then we returned to Coakers' Walk, where we were invited for tea and coffee by Charles's next-door neighbours, also missionaries.

**Author rowing on Kody Lake**

Later, we coasted down on our motorbikes with engines off from the mainly European quarter to the bazaar and found somewhere for lunch. We explored a bit and then it started raining.

At four, we called at the hotel.

"Dhobi still not come, sir!"

We went to his house.

"Clothes not dry – raining, sir!"

"It rains every afternoon here," said Dave.

I took the wet clothes and paid him. Back at the hotel, I found he had burnt a large hole in my shirt and broken the "Levi" button of my jeans.

Dave and Neils were heading back down the ghats to Madurai. They both had work in the morning. The Heinemanns had invited me to stay a couple of nights with them so Dave dropped me off. Charles and his wife went out to dinner, their cook prepared food for me and I had an early night. I was feeling rather lousy.

I was woken in the early morning by a vivid dream in which I was having a crap.  I quickly realised that this had started for real and only just made it to the bathroom.  I was having an attack of dysentery – very violent at first.  Mrs. Heinemann gave me some medicine and sent me off with directions to the Cottage Hospital.  Here I produced a stool sample for analysis and the lab assistant let me look at it under the microscope.  I had a parasite called giardia.  The doctor prescribed Flagyl which proved not to be available at the pharmacy in Kody, so I bought Mexaform instead and dosed myself heavily with that for the next 24 hours.

The whole atmosphere of the Heinemann's house was strangely redolent of childhood visits to my grandparents in Manchester.  Pre- WW2 gentility and calm, a rather Victorian style of furniture- and the afternoon rain dripping on greenery in the garden.

That evening we talked about Seva Nilayam.  The filming had apparently gone as planned.  But because of the crew's late arrival the water diviner had not turned up, so "Geomantic Research Station Private" had been replaced by John the cook holding a couple of twigs and no-one was any the wiser.  Dora had also sent me a message to thank me for my efforts with the hospital in Madurai.

"Don't worry about the boys," she wrote. "It's not your fault. We do what we can.  If they don't help themselves, we can't do any more."

I remember the Heinemanns as a pleasant, welcoming down to earth couple.  I don't recall any prayers or attempts to convert me.  They went to Church on Sunday, but apart from that, it seems to me that they simply tried to live their faith by making themselves useful to other people.

# 14.   Trichy

Next morning, I was up at 5.30 and Mrs Heinemann made me coffee.  The dysentery symptoms had disappeared, but I was beginning to feel I had caught cold in the cool air of the hills. Charles had lent me a pullover, but it was time to return this, so I put on two vests[17], with layers of newspaper wedged between them.   I wrapped my bedspread round me as a cloak and trotted down to the bus stand with the cook's little boy carrying my bag.  This sounds very colonial, but in those days – and perhaps even today - a middle class Indian would have expected the same service.

The bus crept cautiously down the mountain road, horn blaring before every bend, revealing dramatic vista after vista, first to the left then to the right with not even a white line between the tarmac and the precipice.  Did we really come up this in the dark on motorbikes?  Halfway down, there was a fork in the road and we headed north east towards Tiruchirappalli.

Down in the plain it was very hot and dry – June temperatures often exceed 40°C.   I checked into the Tourist Bungalow and slept till 5, then took the local bus out to the massive Sri Rangam Temple – the biggest in India – on its island in the Kaveri River.

Once again I found the typical pattern of concentric rectangular enclosures  –  the  outer  one 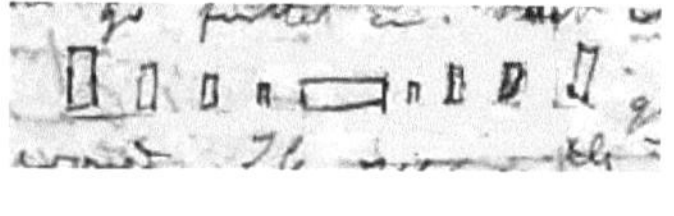 surrounded by a high wall – like a medieval city wall in Europe.

Cars and bullock carts were allowed into the first two courts, which included a big bazaar and living quarters. Then things became more restrictive.  A friendly passer-by swept me past the "Hindus Only" sign saying cheerily, "It doesn't matter!", and was very apologetic when I was politely but firmly asked to

---

[17] Undershirts to American readers.

leave. "You see, they are all Brahmins here," he explained. I was then taken in hand by an old man who negotiated with the gate-keepers to take me a bit further in on condition that he steer me away from the holiest places and prevent me from taking photographs. I see from my diary that this was "quite informative" and cost me one rupee eight annas and a bottle of coke.

Next day I visited the Rockfort Temple complex, perched on its 83 m-high pinnacle above the town. Over the centuries this had been a Hindu temple, a Muslim fortress, a British fortress and had now become a Hindu temple again. From the top there was a good view over the city towards the green island of Sri Rangam, with the gopuras of the temple sticking up above the treetops.

**Rockfort from below**

Trichy did have a pharmacy with Flagyl in stock — the medicine prescribed in Kody to kill my parasites. But it was so expensive that when I got to the station to book my place in the evening train to Madras, I found I didn't have enough money to pay for my berth. Luckily, the clerk was understanding, took my name and kept a berth for me till I could go to the bank and cash some travellers' cheques.

I found Trichy a very dirty, smelly town, with open drains. It was also very hot so I decided I had seen enough and returned to the Tourist Bungalow for an afternoon nap.

The train left at 9.25 pm and I had a place in the 3rd class "three tier" coach, where the bunks fold down on the same principle as in French "couchette" sleepers or Russian "platzkart". But these hard wooden bunks were much smaller. The line from Trichy to Madras Egmore was metre gauge, not the usual broad gauge. At 1m80, I was very tall for India and provided a real pantomime for my fellow passengers as I struggled to fold myself into my short and narrow bed.

## 15.    Madras High Life

We rolled into Egmore Station about 6 am and I waited there till 8 before I started telephoning around.  I had several contacts for accommodation.  The best bet seemed the one Martin had given me back in Bombay – a colleague of his called Stewart at the Oxford University Press.  Imagining him to be in his early twenties like us, I had written ahead a very jokey letter asking him to put me up. Unable to get through by phone, I set out in a rickshaw for the OUP.  When I met Stewart, I found he was "quite old" (at least 40!) and very senior in the O.U.P. hierarchy.  It was obvious that my letter had not made a good impression; he was polite but no, he was afraid he couldn't put me up.

So I went on to plan B and the British Council, where a friendly receptionist phoned a VSO volunteer called Lalage Ann who was teaching at the YMCA P.E. Teachers College.  For once, the call went through without a hitch, Lalage was free and she came straight round to collect me.  She was to introduce me to yet another facet of life in India.

"I can't put you up myself," she said.  "I only have a room at the College Hostel.  But I'll take you round to my friend John's. He's got a big house and he'll be delighted to put you up."

John Comyn turned out to be a very friendly, rich expatriate businessman, living alone -  except for his numerous servants - in a large bungalow surrounded by green lawns.  Short and athletic, he must have been in his forties, but unlike Stewart did not strike me as old.  When I first met him, he was wearing elegant riding boots and if my memory is right, he had just returned from playing polo.

He was indeed delighted to put me up and I stayed for almost a week.  He struck me as being from another age, certainly another class from me.  He had started as a tea planter in Bengal and was now in some kind of import-export business. When he went on leave in the UK, he didn't fly, but usually insisted on going by ship, which was still possible but less and less common.

Like me, Lalage was finding her teaching job unsatisfactory and compensated this by an active social life. Lalage, however, moved in different circles from me. Back in Sagar, my friends and acquaintances were all Indians – mainly students and the younger University teachers and their families. Here, actually living and working in the regional capital of the South, she had been welcomed into the local High Society of expatriates and rich Indian businessmen. It was quite a social whirl. She even had an Indian boyfriend called Derek who had a car – an imported Triumph. A Christian in his early 30's, he had a very good job with Binny's – the textile, shipping and insurance conglomerate founded in 1789 which had played a major role in the economic development of Madras[18]. I noted in my diary that he had a beautiful house, spoke better English than me and claimed to be torn between success and bohemianism – which I considered a load of balls!

For a week, I was invited into this social whirl. I went swimming at the Gymkhana Club, attended the Hot Weather Regatta at the Boat Club – a very leisurely English affair with tea on the lawn, went to the farewell party for the departing British Council Representative – where policemen in Ku Klux Klan-style waterproofs were marshalling the guests' cars through the pouring rain. And I went to several dinner parties and twice to the cinema. Both films were English language – showing Indian audiences alternative views of life in Britain: the blockbuster musical *My Fair Lady* and George Melly's less-known parody of life in "Swinging Sixties" London *Smashing Time* with Rita Tushingham and Lynn Redgrave as two innocent young girls "up from t'North". The only time I had to stay in – because the

---

[18] Finally closed down in 2001 :
http://www.thehindu.com/thehindu/mp/2001/11/12/stories/2001111
200120300.htm

evening was black tie and I wasn't equipped, John left his servants to feed me and ply me with beer.

**Hot Weather Regatta**

At the British Council party, I met another volunteer who was in town for a few days.  This was Chris Gosling from Nagercoil and I was very sorry I had missed him earlier at Cape Comorin. His project was working with the fishermen - trying to introduce the use of outboard motors on those teak-log[19] boats which had so impressed me!  He used to go out to sea with them – said it was quite exciting – you had to leap out of the way if ever the heavy boats turned over to avoid being battered to death!  I'd have loved to have gone with him!

As with us in Bombay, the Council in Madras had paired up each of its volunteers with an expat British "host family" in the city.  Chris was spending a few days with his family, the Marshalls, having covered the 700 km on his motorbike. Mr. Marshall, another senior manager at Binny's, offered to drive me home to John's. On the way, we stopped off at the Gaylord Restaurant and he bought us all steaks.  A band was playing and Mr Marshall found it too loud for his taste and had it quietened

---

[19] Did Chris tell me they were teak?  At Kanyakumari I wrote that they were made of palm-trunks.  Which was right?

– and we then watched a rather abortive strip-tease – not my idea of India at all!  Chris, however, was my idea of a volunteer. We got on well and met up a couple of times during the week, riding around town on his motorbike.

I also did serious sightseeing, some with Lalage, some with Chris, some alone.  One morning, Lalage called fresh from horse-riding and took me to Madras Fort with its museum of British uniforms and portraits of royalty and the 17th century Old Fort Church full of monuments to former British heroes: "Lord So-and-so, Vice Admiral of the Red, Commander of the China Sea, etc."; It was quite a shock coming out of the Fort to realise that India was now in fact independent.

I was struck by a colonial style incident in the Church.  An Englishman bought a guide book from the book-stand, but wouldn't trust the museum curator with the money, so popped his five rupees into the donations safe instead.  This obviously distressed the old man, whose end of day accounts would be five rupees short.  I recounted this to John later.  It turned out he is a trustee of the Church and he said he would make sure the curator didn't get into trouble.

Another time, with Derek we visited the Chola Mandal artist's colony on the beach.  We were shown round the workshops, the artists' huts … and the director's mansion.

On Sunday I took a bus ride out to the temple complex on the beach at Mahabilipuram 60 km south of Madras. This amazing collection of cave carvings, monolithic temples and free-standing statuary has since been declared a UNESCO World Heritage site.   In my day, access was completely open and the atmosphere very informal. The site wasn't crowded, and everyone wandered around, looking, touching, sitting on the monuments…

Monolithic temples and statues

Nandi and calf (Ride-a-cock-horse...)

**Monolithic temple**

**Shore temple**

**Author and friend**

I toured the site with a couple of Indians I had met on the bus, taking lots of photos, swarming over the rocks and paddling in the sea. We got into conversation with a middle-aged American who was walking with sticks. He was a University professor on a study tour and I was intrigued to learn that a couple of weeks earlier he had been at Sagar University – staying in my room at the Guest House and looked after by my servant Lalgi. Once again:

"Small world!"

Madras is also a place of pilgrimage for Indian Christians. Legend has it that St Thomas the Apostle – the one who wouldn't believe Jesus had risen from the dead until he put his finger in the wounds – went to India after the Ascension and was martyred there on a hillock called St Thomas Mount, near the modern international airport. I took the electric train out to Mount Station, walked about a kilometre then climbed the steps up the hill, past the Stations of the Cross. The Church was locked, so I rang the bell of the convent. A nun opened the

Church for me and showed me round.  She showed me the stone on which Thomas had died, a painting of the Blessed Virgin Mary, which she claimed had been painted by St Luke, and another painting of the martyrdom.  She told me Thomas had run here to die after being attacked at prayer in a cave at the Little Mount.  This struck me as implausible as the latter was 6 km away – I walked there later.  She also showed me round the very modern orphanage for babies, sold me some souvenir photos and gave me coca cola to drink.

From the Mount there were fine views over Madras and what was then only an aerodrome.

# 16. Hyderabad Public School

On Wednesday 26th June, I thanked my host, tipped his servants 15 rupees – they were pleased - and set off by the 13.25 train for the fifteen-hour journey to Hyderabad.  I had previously arranged by telegram to stay with a volunteer called Rosemary Davenport, who was teaching in a boarding school there.

Unable to book a sleeping berth, the best I could manage was a seat in the two-tier coach, where there were three overhead berths for every eight seats.  But after my experience in the metre-gauge train from Trichy, I was delighted to be back in broad gauge.  There was plenty of room and when night came, I was able to stretch out for a tolerable night on the floor. During the day, I watched India drift past the window, chatted to fellow passengers, read a *Life* of Martin Luther King and C.S. Forester's *African Queen.*  I also joined in the general complaints about the lousy train meal (<u>and</u> expensive at Rs1.87!) and managed to smash the "unbreakable" Hammer-master thermos flask I had bought in Madras just by knocking it over.

The train made a half-hour breakfast stop at Hyderabad's twin city – or suburb - of Secunderabad .  I found a telephone and called Rosemary.  She was glad to hear me.

"Don't go into Hyderabad.  Get off the train now and take a rickshaw!  You're quite close."

So I went back for my bags, to the confusion of the ticket collector, "Sir, you are booked to Hyderabad.  This is not Hyderabad.  Is Secunderabad…."

The city of Hyderabad had been the capital of a large princely state of the same name ruled by a Muslim dynasty of Nizams.  It had covered large parts of the States I knew in 1968 as Maharashtra, Mysore and Andhra Pradesh.  At Independence in 1947, the seventh Nizam – absolute ruler and reputed the richest man in the world - declared his intention to be even more independent – and not join the Indian Union!  This situation didn't last long.  The Indian Army invaded this landlocked State within a State in 1948 and the Nizam capitulated, though keeping the title of "Princely Governor" until 1956.  By my time, the States had been reorganized and Hyderabad was capital of Andhra Pradesh[20].

Rosemary was teaching at the Hyderabad Public School in Begumpet. This was (and still is) a Public School in the British sense: i.e. a high class fee-paying private school.  The buildings were palatial, the playing fields vast and the institution had originally been built in the 1920's as a school for Muslim princes. All the boys wore a quasi-military uniform.

One might question the use of volunteers to educate westernized elites in Third World countries, but Rosemary loved her work.  She was one of the most satisfied volunteers I met. The school was well organized under its Headmaster Mr Jacob, she had a full timetable teaching primary classes English and was doing a job she knew how to do.  Here we were already in term time and I watched a couple of her lessons with bright, well-behaved, motivated children.

She had a nice room in the teachers' house and for the first few nights I was allowed to use a vacant room there.  Her next door neighbour was a young teacher called Vimla, daughter of a former colleague of my colleague Dr West at Sagar (how many more times am I going to write "small world"?).  As a child, Vimla had accompanied her parents and Dr West on Geological field trips to Bhutan and Tibet.

---

[20] Since re-divided into A.P. and Telengana.

**Rosemary's school**

Here I saw the sights, ate well, went to parties, and drove round in Rosemary's American boyfriend Jim's Mercedes. While I was there, we were visited by another VSO, Gareth Thomas who had been in a sketch with me at the briefing course concert in Tottenham. He was doing research at the Schieffelin Leprosy Research Sanatorium in Karigiri – an institution which has since become a major centre for the study and control of this disease.

It seemed to me that these Madras-based volunteers I met formed much more of a community than those of us in the Bombay "region". They kept in touch much more and many of them had been up to Kashmir together in the summer.

As in Madras, I did quite a bit of partying – this time with a mixed group of Western volunteers and their Indian friends – one of whom, a certain Kapur – surprised me by performing *puja* for the safety of his motorbike! Jim had a party round the pool at his house – the first time I had been dancing since I came to India.

Together we drove out to the fortress of Golconda overlooking the town of Hyderabad. Much of this immense ensemble – known as the ancient centre of the diamond trade - is now in ruins, but the fortifications are impressive. I was particularly struck by a serpentine triple gateway through the thick curtain wall.

**Ruins of Golconda citadel**

We visited a Hindu shrine at the top of the fortress. After performing puja, it was necessary to adjust the red *gulal* marks on our foreheads.

**Gareth, Rosemary and Vimla at Golconda – adjusting *gulal***

After four days, I had to give up my room at the school.  A new teacher was arriving from America.  I saw her drive in with Mr Jacob, the Principal.  A young woman who looked terrified! As for me, I moved out to the tourist bungalow and spent the next couple of days sightseeing and spending what was left of my money on souvenirs.

With Gareth, I made the obligatory visit to the Charminar – the 16th century monument with four minarets which is to Hyderabad what the Eiffel Tower is to Paris and whose picture decorates the cigarette packets of the same name throughout India! We climbed to the balconies above the arches and had splendid views out over the city.

I also spent some time in the city's Handicrafts Emporium. Hyderabad had been for centuries a centre for traditional Mughal arts and handicrafts.  I was impressed by two of these. The first was Bidri - black gun-metal inlaid with silver.  I bought a couple of ash-trays, cuff-links and small boxes.

And then there was Nirmal – delicate painting on specially prepared wood.  Does this still exist?  I find no trace on internet, but I still have two beautiful plates. I didn't have enough cash to buy them, but committed myself to spending two weeks' salary to have them sent by post. I was doubtful about them arriving in Sagar, but they did! In any case, there was no risk for me as it was "Cash on Delivery".

I visited the workshop and saw the many stages of manufacture – the wood-turning, the smoothing, painting and polishing of the plates till they resemble black porcelain, then the delicate painting of the image and a final coating of varnish. Outside in the street, workers were demonstrating with signs saying, "Help the Dying Nirmal Art and Starving Artisans!" and demanding a pay rise.

The plates are 18cm across.  Note the fine brushwork in this enlarged 2cm x 2cm detail of the prince's beard:

**Nirmal brushwork**

My diary also records me buying a set of coffee cups at the Handicrafts Emporium and I still have the set of green hand-painted cups I have always told people I bought in India.  But here is the mystery: they are all stamped "Vallauris" on the bottom and, as my French wife Carole pointed out when she first saw them in 1981, this is the small town on the Côte d'Azur known for its hand-made pottery – and as a one-time home of Picasso, who learnt his ceramic skills there.  Whether genuine or counterfeit, what were these cups doing in a local handicraft emporium in India?

On my last evening in Hyderabad, I went to the cinema and saw *Lawrence of Arabia*.  The audience broke into raucous laughter and cheering when Peter O'Toole, in full Bedouin gear and holed up in a mountain cave, took a roll of toilet paper out of his bag.  Was this a deliberate cinematic comment on his incomplete cultural assimilation?

# 17.Home again, home again, jiggety-jig!

Much of the next day was spent arranging my departure. I sent a telegram to Sagar to announce my imminent arrival. And with the help of a bookseller with whom I had become friendly and his railway contacts I managed to book a berth in the two-tier coach, even though I had been told at the station that, "All is full. Sorry, sir!" There was of course a favour in return: "You will please put in a good word for my cousin who is applying for Sagar University?" It was also in this bookshop that I met a young man who wanted me to tell him "all about sex in England!" He left me rather at a loss for what to say.

I got in at Hyderabad main station and our coach was fairly empty, but at Secunderabad, as I put it, "All hell swarmed on board". We left at 10.30 pm and I would spend all night and all the next day in this train. Luckily, I had brought plenty of reading material. As we headed North, I was surprised to find how pleased I was to see the M.P. countryside again after such a break in the tropical South

As one might expect (small world...), there was someone I knew in the coach – a research student called Bais from my department at Sagar. We had lunch and dinner together in the train and got down together at Bina Junction at 11 pm. Our train was going on to Delhi and we had to wait till 5 a.m. for the branch-line train to Sagar. I lay down on the concrete platform wrapped in my blanket and managed to get a little sleep.

On the local train, a group of "find-the-lady" tricksters got on at one station – a dealer and two stooges. One stooge made it obvious he was bending down the corner of the prize card to mark it – but all the corners were nicked and the player shifted the dog-ear round. They made about 25 rupees from the other passengers then got down at the next station. I found I could follow the cards almost every time, but I didn't take part.

I had never thought Sagar would seem like home, but it did! We took a tonga to Bais's home in the Cantonment, where we had tea, then I went up to the University in a Tempo – the three-wheeler, seven-seat vehicle powered by what sounded like a chainsaw which served as taxi in Sagar – and also provided an unofficial local bus service.

My manservant Lalgi was glad but surprised to see me. As he hadn't been warned, he hadn't got my room ready or any food in. He was looking after a visiting American botanist called Packer, who invited me to lunch and to a party he was holding in the Guest House that evening. I then went to the Office for my pay cheque and called on Dr Mohan Lal, my head of department. He too was surprised to see me. The telegram I had sent from Hyderabad two days earlier was delivered with the morning's mail as we were talking.

So I had arrived again at Sagar for my second year of teaching. But I was no longer the innocent who had arrived the previous August. Now I knew how things worked and I had my network of friends. My recent travels had also widened and deepened my knowledge of India. Perhaps most important, I was arriving before the beginning of term whereas in 1967 I had been slotted into a timetable which was already operating. I was about to take part in the selection of students and in timetable negotiations.

But that is for another volume!

# A note on illustrations

With the exception of the "Charminar" cigarette pack and the poster for the film *One Million Years BC,* all illustrations are my originals: ink drawings scanned from my diary or letters, photos taken by me – or of me with my camera.

1968 was pre-digital, pre-smartphone, pre-selfie.

I went to India with a second-hand 35mm camera with a 50 mm lens whose make I forget.  Focus, aperture and shutter speed were all manually adjusted.

Film was expensive and colour film hard to come by.

For colour, I used Kodachrome II Daylight film at 25 ASA.  This had to be sent to Bombay or London for processing and gave 35mm colour slides.  Black and white was usually Ilford – and could usually be developed locally.  All my India photos were converted to digital form professionally in France in 2012.

One roll of film took 36 pictures.

I set off for the 10-week voyage recounted in these pages with one roll of colour film.  When that was finished, I replaced it with B&W – twice if I remember right.  On average 10 photos per week!  One didn't just shoot away!

The photos of my nirmal ware plates (p. 116) were taken with a small digital camera in 2015.

9 791096 332038